GETTING INTO HEAVEN --

DATE DUE   *in*

GETTING INTO HEAVEN—
and Out Again

Albrecht H. Gralle

Translated by Friederike Gralle
Illustrated by Sally Blakemore

ff

Swedenborg Foundation Press
West Chester, Pennsylvania

Originally published in German as *Wie Sie garantiert in den Himmel kommen—und auch wieder heraus*, © 2007 by Aussaat Verlag, Neukirchener Verlagsgesellschaft mbH.

Library of Congress Cataloging-in-Publication Data
Gralle, Albrecht.
  [Wie Sie garantiert in den Himmel kommen und auch wieder heraus. English]
  Getting into heaven—and out again! / Albrecht Gralle ; translated by Friederike Gralle ; illustrated by Sally Blakemore.
      p. cm.
  Includes bibliographical references (p. 111).
  ISBN 978-0-87785-344-2 (alk. paper)
  1. Heaven. 2. Future life. 3. General Church of the New Jerusalem—Doctrines. I. Title.
  BX8729.H4G733 2012
  236'.24—dc23
                                2011049361

Edited by Morgan Beard
Design and typesetting by Karen Connor

Printed in the United States of America

Swedenborg Foundation Press
320 North Church Street
West Chester, PA 19380
www.swedenborg.com

CONTENTS

GETTING INTO HEAVEN—
and Out Again

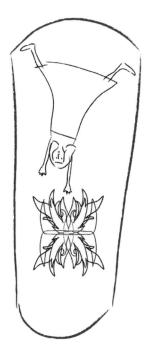

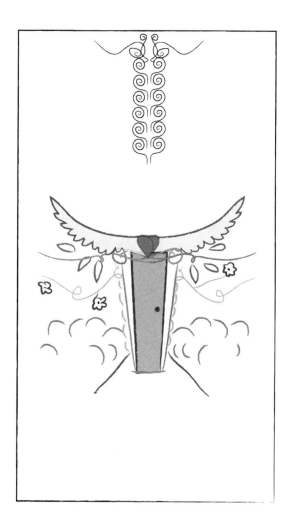

PRETTY SIMPLE

Do you want to get into heaven? Or at least learn how to get there when this mysterious life of ours here on earth is over?

Nothing could be simpler than that.

You can enter heaven any time you like. I don't mean that in the clichéd psychological sense; I'm not going to tell you that "heaven is your inner joy." No, I mean the real heaven, the one your grandparents talked about and wanted to go to, the one the slaves in the cotton fields dreamed about when they sang "Swing Low, Sweet Chariot." They were imagining a heavenly place where you do indeed feel better, where you get a new pair of shoes and jump for joy. A place where you can finally laugh at yourself again, where all wrongs are righted, and your hunger and thirst for justice is finally satisfied.

I mean the heaven where holiness and lust for life aren't mutually exclusive; where there's singing, talking, and planning; where life is finally full and complete.

I do not mean that boring old place where you have to sit on a cloud all day long singing hallelujah with no beer in sight.

Here's the good news: You can enter this real heaven any time. You don't need to be a Christian, a Buddhist, a Jew, a Muslim, or a member of some far-out cult.

Just tell the angel who is guiding you into the otherworld from the hospital where you just died, "I want to go to heaven."

And he'll respond, "Sure, you can go any time you like. I'll accompany you for a while."

At this point, you might be saying to yourself, *Hey, why is this so easy? Why did people on earth make such a fuss about it? Going to churches, mosques, synagogues, temples, or the gym, wrestling with moral issues and commandments and prohibitions and all those deep questions—and now this nice angel is saying, "Just go right in"?*

"Yes," the angel says, hearing your thoughts as loudly as if you were screaming. "God isn't the killjoy you always thought he was. He doesn't deny anyone access to heaven. Here's the entrance. After you!"

He opens a big door. As you might expect, it's a much greater door than anything on earth, and it's made of a truly wonderful, pearl-like substance. It's the door of all doors. Maybe you've heard of Plato's theory of forms or read the letter to the Hebrews in the Bible. They both tell us that the otherworld is where things truly exist, and that our world seems like a poor facsimile in comparison.

In any case, the mother of all doors opens and you see a kind of tingly, pearly light glowing behind it. What am I saying? It's more than just a light; it's something you experience with all your senses. It smells fresh, and you can feel it on your skin like dew. Light the way it's supposed to be.

Your eyes have acquired an amazing ability to perceive things, and now you can see beyond the light into heaven itself. In the distance there are majestic houses with fantastic gardens, and you somehow know that in those houses there are people in heated discussions, painters putting up their easels, craftsmen with their woodwork. Closer to the entrance, there's a band on a stage (or is it a string quartet?) playing unbelievably powerful music that will later inspire someone on earth. There are connections, you know.

Lovers pass by. A golden lion plays catch on a playground. You hear kids squealing with excitement. A melody floats through the air, someone singing solemnly in praise of God. Farther away, in an old stucco villa, a feast is going on. You think to yourself, *Awesome! And I'm a part of it.*

You step through the massive gates and are surrounded by that heavenly light. It sparkles like champagne when you breathe it in. Oh, and by the way, at this point you also have a new body. Your former body from good old earth was nothing but a shadow of this one. Shortly after you died, without much ado, your resurrection took place—your resurrection in heaven, that is. *Resurrection now!* Time is irrelevant.

You walk farther and farther. Then your steps start to slow down until you finally come to a stop.

Suddenly you don't feel as comfortable as you did before. Everything is so strangely open. You're standing in some sort of mental pool; your thoughts are being transmitted to others, and you're receiving the thoughts of people passing by. It's impossible to put on any of your usual social masks; you can't pretend or hide. You discover that your thoughts are much clearer and more comprehensive than on earth. It's as if before you only had one-thousandth of a slice of your brain power at your disposal, and now you have the whole pie—with whipped cream. You slowly start to see things that used to seem mysterious to you in a new light. You begin to suspect connections, and you say to yourself, "So that's how it works!" An abundance of knowledge flows into you.

But in spite of all these wonderful things around you, you become increasingly restless and nervous. You begin to understand that you can only live here if you acknowledge God's authority. He seems to be everywhere. With your new mental clarity, you realize how empty your old life was. You remember seemingly irrelevant scenes from your past when your actions were unjust or unkind, and it makes you ashamed. You don't know what to do with that sense of shame. It feels foreign to you.

You break out in a sweat, because you're afraid you don't have the strength to feel the joy that would be appropriate and necessary for this place. You didn't bring enough joie de vivre. Slowly you take a few steps backward. Heavenly life is roaring in your ears and rustling like a creek, pulsating through your veins like liquid gold. You feel exhausted. It's as though you've been left on a mountaintop with an awe-inspiring panorama, but your body hasn't gotten accustomed to the thin air and its lower pressure yet. You're about to black out.

You look for something to hold onto, and luckily you can feel the shoulder of your friendly angel. He takes your arm and supports you as if you were learning to walk for the first time. You step over the threshold of the gate again, still completely out of breath, only slowly regaining your strength. Thankful for the reprieve, you look at the world outside of heaven. It's an in-between realm, a landscape that's supposed to ease the transition from death to life and better equip you for your current situation. Some people call it paradise. It's a beautifully designed reception area for new arrivals—kind of like the foyer of a vast mansion.

"Phew," you whisper. "That was close."

"If you'd stayed in heaven any longer," the kind angel says in a more personal tone of voice, "I'd have had to carry you outside like a wet sack."

Then he introduces himself. "I'm Bythe, your angel."

"Bythe?"

"Yes. It's short for Taking-You-by-the-Hand. But that's just the name I'm using for this book. My real name is different, and only God and I know that one."

"Strange custom!" you observe.

"It's for protection," Bythe says, "so the people who were celebrities on earth aren't constantly harassed by visitors."

"Maybe they want to be harassed."

"At first maybe, but after three hundred years it can get a little old."

"But . . . don't angels normally have wings?"

"We don't need wings."

"But all those pictures . . ."

"Oh, those." Bythe nods understandingly. "I see what you mean. When we appear on earth we sometimes have wings, but they're only symbolic wings, expressing our lightness."

As the two of you talk, you're recovering a little from your heavenly outing. You say to Bythe, "Geez, heaven just about knocked me out!"

"I knew that'd happen," your angelic companion says. "But you wanted to go so badly. Or the man writing this book wanted you to go so badly. In any case, I think it's an experience you had to go through. Now hopefully you understand that one needs to prepare for heaven, right?"

You nod. "Yes, that's clear. But how do you prepare yourself for it?"

Bythe, who knows your life like the back of his hand, guides you toward a little garden restaurant. He orders two beers—one for you and one for him—and some hearty sandwiches to help you regain your strength. "In order to live in heaven you have to acknowledge that God exists and that everything comes from him," he says. "For example, you have to love openness and admit that you've made mistakes in your life. On earth this is called confession. A boring word. You see, in order to be able to endure the glories of heaven you need to become new from the inside out, or be born again. You have to have heaven inside you if you want to enjoy the heaven outside."

You let the angel's words linger, thinking that they seem logical. You're also thinking that a beer and a sandwich have never tasted this good. You start feeling strong again, and you don't understand why you got so weak in heaven. And that thing about God, about openness and the sin situation and your inner heaven—you'll have to think that through. You ask yourself if you'd be able to tolerate a God, or any sort of superior being, who has a say in everything you do.

Lost in thought, you gaze beyond the trees at a vast mountain range on the horizon and jokingly ask your guardian angel, "So, is there any place where you don't have to believe in God?"

"Of course, we have that too."

"Where is it?" you ask, slightly puzzled, thinking to yourself, *Maybe that's the place for me, somewhere not quite as alive and intense, where life is a little slower, a little more fitting for normal people . . .*

"You'll know if it's for you," Bythe says, and you can't help noticing the sad tone in his voice.

"Could we maybe take a trip there?" you ask cheerfully, feeling adventurous.

Bythe sighs. "If you insist, we will."

"Does this place have a name?" you ask. He really isn't much of talker, this angel of yours.

"Yes, it does have a name. It's known as *hell*."

Bythe almost whispers the word *hell*, shivering.

You hesitate before you continue, "And you really think that we could go there now?"

"Yes, of course, I'll take you. We just need to take a few precautions."

Interlude One

An interlude is a pause for reflection. I truly don't want to impose any nonsense on you, or let my imagination run wild, but pivotal questions such as these have to be processed carefully. They need to be examined for their validity with respect to life and to everything that has been said about God and the afterlife. You also might want to find out if there are people who can confirm what

I'm talking about. The bibliography in the back of the book, for example, serves this purpose.

If you're not interested in these philosophical ponderings, then just skip the interludes and continue with your journey through heaven and hell as an entertaining story. But don't come complaining to me later if you get intellectual diarrhea.

How does a normal human being from the twenty-first century end up believing in life that actually exists after death? Or one that exists parallel to our three-dimensional world? Isn't that a little far-fetched?

Until the eighteenth century, most of the people in the world belonged to a major religion, and most believed in a life after death. Of course, the afterlife could take various forms. Traditional religions in Africa and Asia taught that people's ancestors lived on in a different realm after they died. Jews, Christians, and Muslims still believe in an otherworld. Part of this realm they see as a paradise, populated with creatures who, like us, have a free will, a mind, and emotions. On the other hand, they also find it feasible to imagine a place where wicked people suffer for their wickedness.

This other life is supposed to create a kind of balance for the grave injustices we experience here on earth.

Buddhism is an exception because it teaches an eternal reality in which our ambitions, our greed—the insatiable desires that torture us—will finally be at rest. After all of our wanderings, we will reach a state like an ocean of peace and our individuality will cease to exist.

But no matter how different they might be, all of them shared and still share one belief: Life will continue. This world is not everything.

In the Middle Ages it was practically unthinkable for a person in the Western world not to believe in God and heaven and hell.

It was simply inconceivable. One would have laughed hysterically if someone had claimed, "God is just a figment of your imagination, and heaven doesn't exist at all." So just forget all those novels set in the medieval era with some atheist critic roaming the pages. Historical nonsense!

The idea of an intense, individual life after death is not as farfetched as you might think. Up until very recently it was part of our historical tradition.

Now you might be saying, "So what? Humanity has evolved. We've realized that we don't need all this heavenly superstructure or infernal substructure. We're 'enlightened' people who have freed ourselves from such illusions. We're realists who only believe in what we can see, feel, touch, and comprehend."

My math teacher used to say, "All I believe is that a pound of beef makes a good soup." He and others thought that at some point you have to wake up from your safe little dream world and face the hard facts of reality.

How did that come about?

Probably because our former, simple worldview had been shattered. Before Copernicus, the outside world reflected the inside world. Above was the light, the sun, God. Below was the earth, and beneath the earth it was dark. That was hell. Then Copernicus and other scientists discovered that we are living on a rotating globe. Together with other planets, we are circling around the sun. It became pointless to speak of "above" and "below." People started to think to themselves, "If they were wrong about this, perhaps they're also wrong about the spiritual world." God and the angels "lost" their dwelling place, because up until that point the spiritual world had a place inside the material universe. When this model broke apart, people thought everything else would also have to crack.

A gentleman by the name of Ludwig Feuerbach finally claimed that God and the hereafter were projections of our desires. Because we couldn't stand being finite, we invented an infinite divine being. In order to console ourselves when darkness scared us, we invented—as Feuerbach imagined it—a great consoler: God and heaven and all the angels. Our longing for a heaven and for God cannot be satisfied because he doesn't exist. Period. Such is life! The ants you trample to death every day don't complain either.

These arguments made sense to a lot of people, and they adopted Mr. Feuerbach's conclusion that humanity should concentrate fully on itself and on the present.

And so heaven was left to the pigeons and sparrows.

Between you and me, I have tried very hard, but these arguments never really made sense to me. It's like someone saying, "It's understandable that I'm thirsty and have the desire to drink something. But that doesn't mean I can assume that a cool and quiet place exists where I can sit down and have a kind lady put a big glass of orange juice in front of me."

From that point of view, the desire for refreshment is a nice illusion you have to overcome. This place with the waitress and the juice is nothing but a cheap, tacky consolation. No, when I feel thirsty I have to accept the fact that there is nothing to drink and that I will perish in the next few days. That's life. It's cruel. So let's concentrate on the present thirst.

However, you and I know that this cool room with the waitress and the glass of orange juice actually do exist. If you replace physical thirst with a thirst for life, you might be thinking, *Maybe the idea that my thirst for life will one day be satisfied isn't so absurd after all!*

As Pascal Mercier once wrote, "If it is true that we only live a part of what is in us—what happens to the rest?"

This is definitely a worthwhile question. So then, let's leave Mr. Feuerbach to die of thirst, since he believes that great restaurants with drinks are illusions. Instead, let's say, "At least no one can convincingly prove that God, heaven, and hell don't exist."

Speaking of hell, you were just about to take a trip there. Have fun! 🌱

OFF TO HELL . . .

When I say trip, what I really mean is flight. Yes, in the otherworld you can fly. Without wings. What's the use of wings in a spiritual world with different concepts of time and space?

Bythe takes your hand. You float over some trees. The garden restaurant is to the left below you, and you feel like you're in a Marc Chagall painting. Your clothes change into a luminous blue. You fly straight ahead, across forests, gardens, and fields of wheat, until you reach a stone pit that looks like a quarry. A tunnel opens near the bottom, and a queasy feeling washes over you. But Bythe's grip is strong. You nosedive to the ground and land in front of the mouth of the tunnel.

"This is one of the entrances, if you want to go down," Bythe says.

"Wait—down?" you ask, puzzled. "Why is there an up and down in the spiritual world?"

"Above and below are internal conditions representing spiritual distance. Every inner state in this place seeks an appropriate form. The further we move away from God, the tighter and darker it gets. Here, the weather and the landscape respond to your inner life."

Just like in some cheesy novel? you think. You seem to understand less and less the longer you stand there. "How is it that we've moved away from God?" you ask. "He wasn't in that restaurant, was he?"

Now Bythe has to laugh, and his laugher shakes the ground, knocking a couple of rocks loose. They fall nearby.

"God is everywhere. If he wasn't here, this whole world would dissolve into dust, even the material universe you grew up in. Everything is connected."

You need a couple of minutes to digest the statement, but there's no turning back now. Only one last question. "Can I . . . get out of hell again?"

Bythe nods. "Yes, if you stay close to me. Besides, you're still too immature and unprepared for hell. You'd be spit out again."

"What?" You're surprised. "You need to prepare for hell, too?"

"Of course," your guardian angel says. "Heaven and hell are ultimate states. You need to be prepared for them. Ready? Let's go!"

He takes your hand again and leads you into the tunnel. Darkness surrounds you, and only a faint glow from Bythe sheds light on your path.

The deeper you descend, the more sickening the smell gets. It's like a men's bathroom where the janitor has been on strike for too long. You don't really feel like going on, but Bythe says, "We're almost there. We'll be in the upper region open to visitors. Or, to put it another way, we'll be in the moderate hell, which is the bottom branch of that transitional world you saw when you first arrived. What did you call it? The Foyer. The deep, real hell is not recommended for visitors at all."

Interesting, you think, but you find yourself distracted by the horrible stench. "How can anyone live in a place that smells like this?"

"That's not a problem for the residents here. To them, the smell is pleasant. Just think about dogs. They seem to love bad smells—they go crazy over them."

You turn a corner, then go up a flight of stairs. A morbid landscape unfolds in front of you. It might be appealing to someone who loves the dark and melancholic.

Bythe pulls two long, black cloaks and two dark, wide-brimmed hats out of nowhere and says, "Let's put these on so we don't stick out."

You follow a street that leads to a marketplace. A couple of well-dressed men and women sit around picnic tables counting money.

You join them. Bythe whispers, "Ask them something."

You clear your throat and say, "Hello!"

The woman next to you, who appears to be around fifty and not terribly attractive, looks up in surprise, then says, slightly irritated, "What do you want?"

"I'm just traveling through, having a look around. I've got a couple of questions."

"Ask me," an old man with a crinkly face next to her says. "She's still counting money. I'm done with my first shift. Do you have any money? I could count it for you." Desire glistens in his eyes. You want to be nice to the man, so you reach inside your pocket and are surprised to find a couple of silver coins. You put them on the table. The woman shoots a quick glance at them, her lips moving without making a sound. The man starts to count, but stops almost immediately.

"Are you kidding me?" His voice sounds agitated.

Somewhat insecure, you glance at the table and see that your coins are made of wood, even though they had been silver before.

He throws the coins on the ground. Some dogs wolf them down, but immediately cough them up again.

Finally, you bring yourself to ask a question.

"Do you believe in God?"

"God?" The first man starts laughing, a kind of neighing laughter. "What is 'God'? That's just a word! God doesn't exist. A delusion! Something for the simple-minded."

"And the world, the universe? Where does all this come from?" you ask. It's strange to find yourself taking a position you had never considered before.

"What? Where it comes from? It's always been here. And we built the houses ourselves. What a weird question."

In the meantime, the woman has finished counting the money and looks at you, interested. If you're a man, she'll go on to sit on your lap and start unbuttoning your shirt. She seems to be the kind who doesn't waste any time. If you're a woman, one of the men will hit on you and try to take you to one of the houses nearby.

Their aggressive moves make you uncomfortable, because they're missing even the slightest hint of affection or love. On earth you never experienced anything to this extreme. There was at least a little bit of affection, even from the most die-hard egotists. It gives you the shivers, banishing any erotic feelings you might have had. Besides, the odor emanating from these would-be lovers is nasty. It smells like a chicken coop on a rainy day.

Bythe gets up, pulling you up as well. In doing so his cloak shifts a little, and a beam of heavenly light flashes across the group. You jump up, frightened, because all of a sudden you're surrounded by monsters: half-animal, half-human, hairy creatures with claws on their hands and flames between them. Paintings from Hieronymus Bosch come to mind. You run away screaming. Behind you, you hear someone calling, "Stay here. You can count money all day long and have fun. Life is glorious!"

You stop running just outside the village, near a boggy marsh. Still a bit shocked, you ask Bythe, "What was that?"

"Oh that! Heavenly light shows what the people in hell are really like. God lets them live with their illusions, so that they aren't tortured by their real personas."

"Then God is present even in hell?"

"In a way, yes. Indirectly—twisted by the residents, bastardized, and repressed. In these upper levels of hell, his influence is more direct. You know, nothing can exist, not even evil, if it isn't ultimately fueled by divine energy."

All this is completely new. A thought occurs to you. "Then all these—these images of fire and agony . . ."

"Yes?"

"All these images come from the perspective of the heavenly?"

"Correct. From heaven you see the reality, but for the residents of hell it's a continuation of their lives on earth. They tenaciously cling to their favorite pastimes, even if they are terrible. There are deeper parts of hell where they make each other's lives even more hellish, but they don't want it any different."

"Then . . . God lets them lead the life they want?"

"Exactly. If he took away their desire for wickedness, for perversion, for hatred and stench, they couldn't continue to exist. Your affinities make up your life. If someone were to take them away, you'd stop living."

As the two of you talked, you began walking again. You've moved away from the marsh into a grassy area, but the grass is yellow and scrawny. Gaunt trees grow in between the patches. The air is buzzing with mosquitos. Then some houses appear.

Right now, you're not sure if you want to meet any more people down here, but you're curious and, after all, your guardian angel will protect you. That's his job.

It has grown dim. You can see faint lights glowing inside the clay and wood houses.

Bythe knocks on one of the doors.

From the inside you hear an indistinguishable sound. The two of you enter. A dull lamp hangs from the ceiling, illuminating a group of people who are feverishly occupied with drawing something. They are holding small plates in their hands and looking into them.

One of them looks up when the door opens and growls, "Sit down and shut up!"

Slightly intimidated, you obey, and watch what the painters are doing. You realize that they are holding little mirrors in their hands, continuously drawing self-portraits.

Then you have an idea. Because really, you're nobody's fool. You take the corner of your angel's cloak and turn it up. A streak of heavenly light illuminates the room, and you shudder and jump back. In this light the artists look like skeletons with tin crowns on their heads. They're sitting on blocks of ice, freezing. At that moment, you hear a gruesome cry from below, like a scream from a dungeon.

Turning up Bythe's cloak like that wasn't such a great idea. Suddenly the entire group is focused on you. One of the artists, whose corpse-like face is distorted with hatred, jumps up and runs toward you.

Bythe raises his hand and the artist stops, puzzled.

The two of you flee the hut as quickly as possible. Bythe takes your hand again and you shoot up into the air, flying until you reach a summer meadow.

"Hey! Where did hell go?" you ask, breathless.

"Here," Bythe says, and points to a small crack in the grass.

"We were down there?"

"Yes. Hell isn't much compared to reality. Are you still cold?"

"Just a bit."

You walk on until you reach an Alpine lodge with a bench in the sun. Exhausted, you sit down.

Bythe orders hot tea and smiles as he watches you drink.

Then you remember something. "That awful cry before, from beneath the ground?"

"That was the deeper hell. The self-imposed suffering of those people is so horrific that it would make the blood in your veins freeze if you visited them there."

As you slowly regain your strength, you think about the contrast: Even if heaven knocked you out, on the whole it was a lot more pleasant up there. You even feel a slight longing for heaven, just for the balance.

Then you have another idea.

"Tell me something, Bythe," you say. "Couldn't I take the cloak and hat we had and go into heaven? Then the light and the air wouldn't be so hard to bear, and I could have a better look around."

"I'll ask the boss about it," Bythe says. He sits quietly for a moment, seemingly listening to some internal voice. "OK, you've got permission. But we'll need a different cloak and hat. We need something white, reflective. Makes sense, doesn't it?"

# Interlude Two

"Hell," the existentialist Jean-Paul Sartre once said, "is other people." He meant that we can make each other's lives hell, and that hell starts here on earth, just as heaven does.

Maybe you got a strange sensation during those scenes in hell and were thinking, "We finally got rid of our fear of hell and now Gralle comes along and starts it all over again!"

Are there any scenarios more horrific than Auschwitz? Why do we need a hell in the afterlife? Wouldn't it be so much better if everything just ended after death? Isn't it enough to have turned this earth into hell? And don't we believe in a God of love? How could he stand to have his creatures rot in hell?

Don't these ideas about hell originate from an ancient worldview that we can confidently put aside?

I have tried to describe the common conceptions of hell in a different way, namely, as a logical consequence of the way we live our lives. This is not my idea, as you will see in the books listed in the bibliography.

Believe me, God doesn't enjoy punishing anyone for anything. He's no sadist. We punish ourselves if we move away from God, who is the source of life.

But if we assume that a spiritual life exists even after the earthly body dies and that we will continue there, then we also have to assume that we will be the same person there—we can't suddenly just become someone else.

"Man, you will be transformed into what you love," writes the famous poet Angelus Silesius, suggesting that our lives are intrinsically connected to our fundamental loves. One could also quote the words of the famous Swedish natural scientist and universal genius Emanuel Swedenborg: "I am that which I love. My basic affinity is the core of my essence."

Every person—if they are being honest with themselves—has a hidden or open passion flowing through his or her life like a deep river. Everything we do, say, or initiate is fed by this fundamental love.

One person might have an inner urge to do research or teach; another has a love of children or enjoys inventing things; and yet another is completely taken by music, or her life is dedicated to agriculture—sowing, growing, and harvesting. There might be someone who loves nothing more than helping others or reforming things. Someone else just simply loves leading a normal life and having a big family.

But there are also people who enjoy doing evil, torturing others, stealing, deceiving, and killing. It gives them their greatest pleasure. They would never openly admit to it, because it is not well looked upon, but inwardly all their thoughts and desires are directed toward this activity.

If you take away people's basic affinities, their lives will be destroyed. They will stop being themselves, even if what they love isn't conventionally considered "good" and is destroying them.

Life after death consequently seems to let us retain these basic affinities. And hell would be the only place where someone who loves nothing more than stealing and lying and perversions, and who hates others, would be in good hands. He could never exist in heaven because the whole atmosphere would be working against him.

So he lives in a spiritual world with others who are like him. They make each other's lives hell and enjoy it up to a certain point. At the same time, they suffer because of each other. This kind of life barely deserves the name.

And if you multiply that one person's experience by the countless number who have that kind of life and love, you'll have an idea of what hell is like.

God allows everyone to lead the kind of lives they created for themselves. He doesn't need to punish. Sin, a self-imposed distance from God, is itself a punishment.

For heaven's sake! Is there no getting away? Does hell never end?

Hell here on earth can end when people turn to God and ask him to save them from these compulsions and fundamental affinities. This is called "repentance," or being born again, and it is often a painful process. God has to penetrate our very core and change it with his positive energy and spirit. That is only possible if we chose it freely. Otherwise God would be destroying our freedom.

The whole process is a gift God is offering us. You cannot earn God's affection or buy it. In the same way, you cannot earn your admission into heaven by doing pious deeds. Everyone can enter. However, in order for our lives to lead us to heaven, we need to let God work in us.

And by no means do all people who call themselves Christians automatically get into heaven and all the non-Christians end up in hell.

It could be that a Christian's fundamental affinities are hatred and wickedness, even though no other person would ever suspect it. If so, they wouldn't feel comfortable in heaven, but could

really only live in hell. Even if they profess that they believe in the Christian creed, even if they have been baptized or apparently converted.

It all depends on their inner lives.

Therefore, it is no coincidence that Jesus's whole Sermon on the Mount is about changing your inner attitude.

There are probably non-Christians who have served God without knowing it, or ones who have been moving toward him, living in love, and are therefore headed for heaven. The Gospel of Matthew says that Christ will judge every person according to their deeds and motives. He is the one who makes the final decision. The paths to God ultimately lead through him. It wouldn't be such a bad idea to get to know him now.

But let us continue with our story. You were about to borrow a cloak to better endure heaven, but then you think that you're starting to enjoy the Alpine lodge in the Foyer. The view is fantastic. Maybe you don't want to live in heaven after all. Maybe the Foyer will do. That's all you need. And this is what you tell Bythe before he can take you through the door of all doors again . . . 🌟

PARTY WITH ORANGE CREAM CAKE

"Bythe, wait a second," you say. "Before we disappear into heaven again, just one tiny little question: That restaurant and the pretty forest we flew over a while back, and now this beautiful setting here, I mean, honestly, it's not so bad. And I didn't have anxiety attacks. Can't I just stay here in the Foyer? I'm sure it's full of interesting people, too. Orpheus and Eurydike, for example, or Alfred Hitchcock. I mean . . . I was just wondering."

Bythe stops. "I was afraid you would ask me that," he says. Big deal for a guy who can read your thoughts.

"First of all," he continues, "you're going to spend quite some time here after you die, anyway, so that you can be prepared for either heaven or hell."

You swallow hard. "Wait, you mean there's actually a possibility that I'm going to end up in hell, with all those disgusting money counters?"

"I don't know." Bythe shrugs. "Spending a while in the Foyer will tell you who you really are inside. Do you understand? Your inner self has to become your outer self. God wants us to be who we really are—through and

through. That's the goal. One could describe your stopover here with an old-fashioned word, 'last judgment.' Judgment means that a process of separation begins, and that everything that doesn't belong to a person will fall away. Step by step you become what you already are on the inside."

"Hm," you mutter to yourself. "Becoming what you already are."

"Exactly," Bythe says, and pats you on the back. "Everything is about your substance, your primal affinity. In a spiritual world you can only survive when you are completely authentic. You are you. Everything else is window dressing; it doesn't last. Think about it! God went to great lengths to have psychoanalysis develop on earth so people could learn more about who they are. Being authentic, my friend, that's what it's all about."

"Hm." You're really thinking now. "Then why do we need faith and the commandments, when in the end it's all about being authentic?"

Bythe smiles. "Faith and the commandments are the means to accomplish exactly that. If they don't serve life, then they're pointless. So the answer to your original question is this: Once you've pushed through to your inner core, you can't keep living in the Foyer anymore."

"All right," you say. "I'm sure you know what you're talking about. Still, I'd love to stay for a while and take a look around."

"Sure. Please do. Time is no object." Bythe nods, adding, "Here, I'll leave you to yourself. When you're ready, just think about me for a second and I'll be there."

"And . . ." You hesitate a little.

"Yes?"

"And nothing can happen to me here?"

"No. But when you need help, like I said, just think of me."

"But what if I suddenly run into God here?"

Bythe shakes his head. "Don't worry. That doesn't really happen unless a newbie specifically desires it. But we'll get a chance to meet God in heaven later. I guess that's a given, right?"

"Right. So . . . see you later then." You are just about to leave when you remember something. "Am I alone here?"

Bythe laughs. "Everything here is full of people. You just haven't noticed them yet because you were too busy dealing with yourself. There's always someone arriving or on his way to a prep course. You'll see. And you can just ask people anything you want."

With that, Bythe lifts off the ground and flies away.

Just when you begin to wonder where all these people are that Bythe was talking about, you hear a murmur as if from a distant waterfall. You see hundreds or maybe thousands of people all around you, coming from and going to places, standing in groups or sitting and talking. It's a truly idyllic scene. The mountain meadow has gotten wider and turned into a park: majestic oak trees, beeches, and maples grow from the lush grass where people are sitting or lying around. A lake stretches along the border of the park. You randomly walk toward a group of young people who are sitting on the grass and singing a song. They don't seem too intimidating.

"Hello," you say. "May I join you?"

"Of course, please do," a young woman replies. You feel as if you recognize her from somewhere. She gives you a mischievous smile. "There's space right next to me."

You sit down and say to the smiling woman, "This is probably going to sound strange, but you seem really familiar."

The woman laughs. "Of course I seem familiar," she says. "I'm your grandmother, silly."

Your jaw drops an inch. Last time you saw your grandma she was lying in a hospital bed, shriveled up like a dried apple, mumbling incomprehensibly. Now she's looking young and fresh, well groomed and pretty.

In your earthly life you got used to watching people grow older, but it's completely different to meet someone who has grown fifty years younger. You've never seen anything like it.

"Surprising, isn't it?" She laughs.

"It sure is." Only now do you realize that there are no old people at all here. There are children, teenagers, and adults of maybe thirty years, but that's it.

"Are there no old people here?" you ask your grandmother.

"No, we're all in our prime here, except for those who died as children or teenagers. They keep growing. And there are some super-wise people who look a little more dignified. So you just died, then?" she asks compassionately.

You're not really sure how to explain yourself.

"Well, I haven't really died," you begin, "it's more like . . . I'm a possibility, or a character in a story, or something like that."

"I see." Your grandma nods. "Yes, that happens. At least this way you'll kind of know what to expect later. That's not so bad, I guess."

You're actually pretty happy to have met your grandma here. Now you can ask her whatever you want.

"So, tell me, Grandma, have you been here in the Foyer a long time?"

Your grandma shrugs. She seems to understand your nickname for this transitional world. "You know, you kind of lose your sense of time. I've been here since I died. How long ago was that now?"

"It was about twelve years ago."

"See? That's how long I've been here. I really didn't think it had been that long. But I'll tell you what—soon I'll be ready to go to heaven. The first heaven, that is."

"Hey, you made it! Congratulations, Grandma!" you exclaim, and then chatter on, happy to be able show off in front of these people. "Guess what—I've already been to heaven with my guardian angel."

"Really?" The others eye you curiously. And you notice one exceptionally pretty woman among them. Should you be a woman yourself, it would be a handsome man who stood out for you. But since you remember that you can't fool anyone here, you continue, "But . . . well . . . I didn't handle the climate very well and . . . I had to leave right away."

The others in the group nod knowingly. Someone offers you a slice of cake, which you gladly accept. There are no napkins because the cake doesn't crumble. It tastes delicious, like orange cream. And there's no need to worry about your figure. You will only put on weight if it corresponds with your inner self. Remember: Think thin—don't puff yourself up or show off.

Now you're starting to really feel at home in the circle of deceased. Just as you're about to ask another question, a man runs past you, around the tree, looks you in the eye, and runs off again.

"Who was that?"

"Oh, he's a newbie. He died really quickly, probably in a car accident. He hasn't figured out what's happened to him yet. See, his angel is coming. He'll have to carefully break the news to the poor man or take him to the city."

To the city? What's that about? You make a mental note to ask if you get the chance. Now you see a man appear next to the confused guy, put his arm around his shoulders, and say a couple of words to him.

You remember that you had another question, and so you seize the opportunity. "What I was going to ask . . . I was really surprised before when my guardian angel told me so casually that here in the Foyer, you're being prepared for either heaven or hell. Now I'm trying to imagine what it's going to be like if it turns out I'm going to hell. Thing is, I already got a little glimpse of it."

It's silent for a little while, and you start to hear the rushing of the multitude of voices again. The man who offered you the cake says, "We are being prepared here, that's true. But it's a good sign that your immediate reaction was to sit down with us, because all of us here are being prepared for heaven. For Rainer and Claudia, the decision process isn't completely over yet."

"And could someone here tell me the criteria? What makes the difference between going to heaven and going to hell?" As you ask this, you realize that it's a very important question indeed.

"There's not much to say about that," your grandma begins. "First, if you want to go to heaven, you need to acknowledge that there is only one God."

Of course I have no idea what you are thinking right now. I don't know if you're an atheist, a Muslim, a Jew, a Christian, or whatever else there might be. But for argument's sake we will assume you're a kind of sympathetic theist.

"And the second thing," your grandma says, "is that you will also have to accept in some way that God revealed himself to us as a human being."

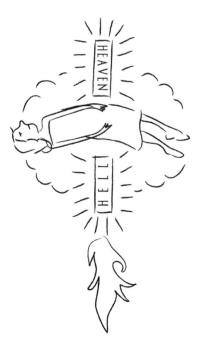

"As a human being? What's that supposed to mean?" you ask.

"Well, let's put it this way," the cake distributor explains. "It isn't really possible to properly imagine God. He's just too big. Someone who created the universe and is present in every part of it doesn't exactly fit into our imagination. It's just like with ants."

"Ants?"

"Yeah, ants can crawl up and down your body, but they will never be able to fully grasp you."

"True."

"That's why—a long time ago, in human terms—God came to earth as a child, making himself comprehensible. Since then, we can at least look at him without fainting right away."

"You could say that he came as an ant," your grandma adds. "The ant can't see you the way you are unless you yourself become an ant."

"Ah, I see," you say, "the incarnation! You mean Jesus Christ. Next you're going to say that the Christians were right all along and the others weren't. Help! I've ended up in a Christian propaganda book!"

The people next to you on the grass all start laughing as if they'd heard the best joke ever.

You are slightly annoyed.

Your young, good-looking grandma puts her arm around you and kisses you on the cheek. "Isn't he just sweet?" she tells the others. Or if you're a woman, she might say something like, "Isn't she just adorable?"

"Why?" you ask, bewildered. "Did I say something wrong?"

"Maybe a little," your grandma says. "Look. Of course, God actually did live and suffer through a whole human life, with all the good and the bad. Then finally he was killed, and went on to kill death itself in order to make it possible for us to be resurrected. That's the whole reason why we can get into heaven in the first place, because God as a human being cleared away all the obstacles. Since that day everyone can return to God. There's no getting around that fact if you want to get into heaven. This is the only way. No one gets to the father except through the son. But— my goodness, that doesn't mean that everyone who can recite the Christian creed automatically gets into heaven. I assume your guardian angel already told you that all that matters is the inside, the core."

You nod. "Yes, he did."

"There are many Christians who actually believe the right thing, who are baptized, and who pray to God—but all that won't save them one bit if all they have inside them is a bale of hay. Do you understand? You've got to start with faith, build something with substance, live it on a daily basis, love your neighbor. Repenting of the wrong and turning your life around. To put it bluntly: Thinking instead of mindlessly going through the motions." She lets that sink in. "In the beginning Christians had an advantage, but now some of them have become so self-righteous and arrogant that we have a Christian department in hell. They didn't preserve their heritage well. There are people, as an angel recently told me in class, who spend centuries of the earthly calendar running around in the uppermost level of hell insisting that they have the right to get into heaven because they believed the right thing and converted. But if faith only consists of words and doesn't live in your heart, it isn't worth anything. Faith without actions is dead. They put those know-it-alls into heaven for a bit, just to show them they could never survive with their kind of arrogance. Now they complain that they were being tricked."

"My case was a little different," a man with olive skin says. "I arrived here some years ago as a Muslim. Of course, I searched for the Muslim paradise everywhere. Some of the angels finally brought me to the park here, and I thought that surely Mohammed was going to come around the corner any moment. Eventually they helped me understand that all of that has lost its relevance. My life was tested to see how much I loved, and I had time to think over some things and to turn to God completely. Now I'm one of the next candidates for heaven. Isn't it just crazy that there seem to be completely diffrent standards at work here? Terms like 'righteous' and 'heathen' don't matter when you're about to enter heaven. It's all about your inside."

"Well," your grandma says, "the ones marching into heaven aren't heathens anymore, I guess."

And you start thinking about the song "When the Saints Go Marching In."

"The last will be the first," someone from the group says. And another adds, "Cheers to Ahmed, and international understanding!" Everyone raises their glass except you, because you don't actually have one, and drinks to Ahmed.

"And what about the Arabic suicide bombers?" you ask. "Do they also end up around here somewhere?"

Ahmed gloomily shakes his head and points his thumb downwards. "They are all totally loopy. But as your grandmother said,

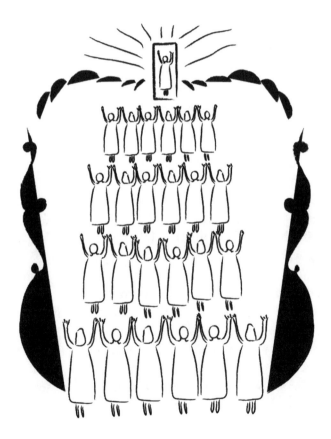

it's all about your inner person. Maybe there are some among them who were just forced to die like that. Naturally that would change things. Maybe they'll get their act together. But you can't be certain. On earth, there's a lot more leeway in making these decisions."

You still haven't totally understood everything, but you have another question, and you figure that it can't hurt to ask. "And why exactly is it so important that God became human?" Ahmed hands you another piece of cake, which you gladly accept.

"Probably because wrong ideas about God can't exist within the heavenly atmosphere," Ahmed explains. "I watched thousands of Christians having to take extra courses because they came here believing there were three gods in heaven: the Father, the Son, and the Holy Spirit. It took them years to get rid of that."

"Fpfill," you say with your mouth full and swallow your cake. "Still, isn't that what they teach in church—the Trinity and so on?"

"The Trinity is all right," your grandma says, getting her knitting gear from her basket. "I'm not a theologian, but as far as I can tell from being here, it's about understanding the three sides of God: the divine, the human, and the active one. You could call that the Father, the Son, and the Holy Spirit, but of course there is only one whole divine being."

For a couple of moments you listen to your grandma's knitting needles clicking. Then she says to you, "I think this might be enough for now. Maybe it was all a little too much for a start. Would you like some white wine?"

"Yes, that's a fantastic idea," you say, even though you've never tried cake with white wine. You take the full glass, smell the wine, taste it, and are overwhelmed by how delicious it is. Amazing! This alone was worth the trip.

After some literally divine sips you start to feel adventurous enough to take another look around this fascinating Foyer.

Interlude Three

I can almost sense that someone has been nervously shifting in his chair for a while now, wanting to interrupt. "Please," I would say to the reader, "just let it all out."

"You're so naïve, Mr. Gralle!" he says. "OK, let's just assume that life goes on after death. It wouldn't happen in a human kind of way, with all the earthly trappings you describe here. We leave

all of that behind us when we die, because we're entering a spiritual world. Tell those stories to your grandchildren, but not to adults who are able to think for themselves."

OK. I hear that, and I ask the loud questioner, Why should a spiritual world be less real than ours? Old Plato and the writers of the letter to the Hebrews and the book of Revelation—all of them find it self-evident that the hereafter is even more real than this world, and that this creation is only a shadow of it. Plato spent a lot of his time thinking, and is still a very well-respected, serious philosopher. And even though the Bible holds back a little when it comes to describing the afterlife or the heavenly realms, it talks about trees, rivers, cities, clothes, music. It talks about being able to eat bread and drink wine in an entirely different way.

In the 1950s, C. S. Lewis, a professor of English literature from Oxford, England, wrote an exciting and ingenious story titled *The Great Divorce*. Absolutely worth a read! He describes heaven as a harder kind of reality. The people arriving need time to get used to the firm blades of grass and heavy water drops before they are able to really enjoy all of it.

"Nonsense! Those are all just metaphors!" the raucous critic might interrupt.

Of course they are. But the metaphors and images help us to visualize. Imagine a river, the way it flows and glistens in the sun, and how refreshing the water is when you get into it. What if I told you that in heaven there is something similar to a river, only much better and more perfect?

The fact that one is using an image or a metaphor doesn't mean that the thing it represents isn't real. Maybe it's we who need to revise our idea of the spiritual world?

Wouldn't a heavenly body at least be able to do everything an earthly body can do, and probably much more? What kind of heavenly body would it be if it didn't have senses, if it couldn't feel, couldn't eat and drink with pleasure, couldn't move; if you could neither see it, nor hear it, nor talk to it? If it only floats around like a waft of mist? A miserable little thing that God would have to be ashamed of.

No, the images and metaphors give us a hint: it's going to be like this, but much better.

"Oh, come on!" I already hear some annoyed person say. "Something inner or spiritual is formless; it's immaterial. You make everything sound too cute, Mr. Gralle, and you press it into a physical mold. But the spirit is completely free!"

I can only respond with Hegel, who spent his life thinking about these things, and finally declared that an inner reality cannot truly exist without an outward manifestation.

He's right, of course. All content needs a form; otherwise there can't be content. Even something spiritual has to find an outward expression. It might be immaterial, but it will still have form. A spiritual human being needs a spiritual body to survive when the other body is lost during the transition to the spiritual world.

But enough of our discussion. Let's return to paradise for a moment. There are a couple of surprises lined up for you.

THE TENT

You say goodbye to your grandmother and her friends and wander on. A new park opens up before you with a huge tent right in the middle of it. As you watch, you see two people carrying a patient on a stretcher into the tent.

Of course you're curious, and you follow the two paramedics. You slip inside the tent, trying not to be seen, and are dumbstruck to find that the inside is vast, much larger than it appeared to be from the outside. It's decorated with beautiful carpets, and there are people lying on comfortable-looking beds with colorful quilts, sleeping—or are they sick? Sometimes people or angels sit next to the beds and hold the person's hand.

Carefully you step closer and ask a woman passing by what this tent is for.

The woman, around thirty and good-looking (of course), pulls up a chair for you and invites you to take a seat. She seems to be some sort of nurse.

"This is the sleeping tent," she says.

"Oh," you say, still not really understanding. "And why are they all sleeping?"

"Some of them are people who've had a very exhausting life and wished for nothing but a chance to rest before dying. That's the lighter category, and they're sleeping over here to my left. Next to them lie the people who have suffered great hardship. Some come from places where there was war or some sort of natural disaster. Many of the children among them were killed by a violent crime. They need a lot of sleep. It's a kind of therapeutic sleep, healing the wounds of their souls. We send them helpful dreams, and after a long time they finally wake up and are able to participate in one of our courses."

"Aha!" you say. "Is this what people mean when they talk about the sleep of death?"

The woman nods her head. "You could call it that, but of course the patients aren't dead. They're only processing the most horrific moments from their lives." The nurse points to the light-colored tent walls. "Look for yourself."

Beside each patient you see a sort of 3D movie with scenes from his or her life. There is a woman who is being raped several times by laughing soldiers and then stabbed to death. It's horrendous. You turn your head away and ask, "And this kind of sleep actually helps?"

"Sure. We let them repeat the experience and soften it a little each time until the negative effects recede. It takes time, though."

"And the soldiers who did this? Where are they? Did they get into heaven, too?" You can hear the irony in your own voice.

"Yes. One of them has a good chance. He radically repented later and truly changed his life. He's really responding to our training sessions. But two of the others were already corrupted in their hearts—they just loved doing evil more than everything else. We weren't able to influence them anymore. You'll probably run into them in hell somewhere."

You thank her and walk on, still slightly numb. The amount of information you have to take in is a little overwhelming at times. You can only stand it here because of the peculiar silence emanating from the tent. It's not an empty, sterile silence, it's an energized silence. It makes sense if you think about what's going on in their dreams. In any case, the silence is contagious. There's a quality about the place that makes you feel as if a happy ending is just around the corner. Although you don't want to admit it, the old cliché that "everything will be fine" may have some truth to it. It actually seems to be right most of the time. Maybe you think, *Why didn't anyone tell me before? It would have spared me so much worrying.*

The further you go, the more amazed you are at how many thousands, if not millions, of people seem to fit into the tent. Every time you think you've reached the end of it, another section reveals itself. Some beds have a nightstand or a wardrobe next to them. Some have framed pictures hanging on the wall, as if the patients were in their normal surroundings. Maybe it's to cushion their transition into the beyond. In the children's beds you see stuffed animals and covers with kid's themes. You almost start feeling tired yourself. And still you haven't reached the end of the tent.

"The inside is always bigger than the outside," someone next to you says, and once again you are reminded that people can hear your thoughts in heaven's never-ending Foyer. You turn around, recognizing the voice. "Bythe! I can't even remember calling you!"

"But I heard you calling me. Maybe it was from somewhere deep within that didn't even reach your consciousness. Apparently, there's a question bothering you, one that you can't quite put into words."

"Maybe you're right. It feels like I'm being bombarded with new thoughts and ideas. But I really like the tent, to be honest. Before, whenever I started thinking about God, I always hit a stumbling block when I thought about the unimaginable state of things on earth. A God who loves the earth and its human beings couldn't possibly allow all of that. That's what I used to tell myself."

As you talk, the two of you leave the sleeping tent, and in a little while you come to an amphitheater. It's beautiful, the way it blends into the landscape, surrounded by cypresses underneath a deep blue sky that reminds you of Greece. The theater is half full, and a scene is being acted out down below on the stage. Curious, you and Bythe sit down and follow the action. Luckily, it's not in Greek.

Just between the two of us: everyone that arrives here speaks a kind of universal language without ever having had to study it.

Interlude Four

Forgive me if I've presumed too much about your beliefs in my book. I've portrayed you as thinking that it is hard to have faith in God with all the suffering we have on earth. But you see, these kinds of ideas are very common, and I assumed you might have had them, too, at times when you were watching the news on television. They're the questions one struggles with when talking about God.

I find it refreshing knowing about those therapeutic tents. It restores a sense of order to the terrible chaos down here. It's important to learn to judge things in relation to how they end; otherwise you just go crazy. The tangled threads on the backside of an oriental carpet only make sense once you turn the whole thing around.

I can already imagine how Mr. Feuerbach would respond if someone tried to tell him about the therapeutic tents. "Really," he'd say. "What's that supposed to be? Sorry to disappoint you, but death is impartial. It crushes everyone, the rich and the poor, the young and the old, the good and the bad. Deal with it! There is no poetic justice! We don't live in a fairy tale where the bad are punished and the good are rewarded. When will those religious weirdos finally get that? We are our bodies. Our bodies and the structure of our brains give us the illusion of an I-consciousness. Got it?"

"My dear Mr. Feuerbach," I'd say. "Think about it for a moment. Are you seriously arguing that something spiritual, something that's eternal, is created from chemical processes?"

"The human mind is not eternal, Mr. Gralle."

"It certainly is, Mr. Feuerbach. In our minds, you and I can advance to the farthest corners of the universe. Given unlimited time, we can imagine infinite worlds. And you claim that an ability as astonishing as this is just going to rot once our body has died? Is there anything more ridiculous than the idea that something immaterial should rot?"

Mr. Feuerbach is silent, and so I continue, "If immaterial life has ever existed outside a material body, then why shouldn't a spiritual world exist where God gives compensation for all the suffering on this earth? It's worth thinking about, isn't it?"

Fortunately, there's another story about suffering that's about to be acted out in the amphitheater. 🌱♡

THE ACCUSED

Down on the stage of the amphitheater, a man with ropes binding his hands is standing in front of a judge, who is addressing him reproachfully. "You're being accused of not taking care of humankind," he is saying. "I have a big stack of letters here from people with bitter complaints. I'll just read you a sample. . . ."

"Who is the accused?" you ask.

"It's God," Bythe whispers, "or rather, an actor playing God."

"This letter is from a ten-year-old boy," the judge continues. "'Dear God, why did my parents have to be shot right before my eyes? Why did you allow that? That was really mean of you.'" He puts the letter aside and takes the next. "'Dear God, I waited sixteen years for my son to come home, and then I got a note saying that he died in the war and was buried somewhere without a funeral. How can they be so cruel? Why didn't you do something?'"

The prisoner stands in front of the judge without moving, just listening to him.

"'Dear God, I never had a chance. The others were always better than me. I was unemployed for eight years. Couldn't you have found me a job? You are all-powerful, aren't you?'"

"'Dear God, my sister was always prettier than me. The men always chased her. I think it's unfair that I have acne all over my face and am heavier than her!'"

The judge's voice is getting louder as he reads, and quietly you think to yourself, *The letter writer actually has a point there.*

"'Dear God, I am only five years old and had to lie in a dark hole for two weeks. A man pretended I was a grown-up woman. He breathed heavily and groaned all the time and it hurt a lot. Then he let me starve to death. I'm still really sad.'"

The pile of letters on the table in front of the judge hasn't gotten any smaller. But God is just standing there, saying nothing. You're getting a bit annoyed, and you think, *If God created a world with human beings, he really could have made it so that things run a little more smoothly.*

"'Dear God,' someone writes, 'yesterday I sprained my ankle just before the race and couldn't run. It's not fair! I'm sure I'd have won. One year of training for nothing. You messed everything up.'"

"'Dear God, yesterday my whole village was destroyed by bombs, and now our neighbors are a pile of blood and bones. What do you say to that?'"

"Yes," the judge says, looking up from the letter. "That's what I'd like to know. What do you have to say to that, Accused?"

Silence comes over the assembly, and you notice that you're biting your lip. What will the convict say?

Of course, you know about the therapeutic tents now. But couldn't he have prevented most it before it ever happened? Why did there have to be so much pain and suffering in the first place?

The accused still hasn't said anything. Instead he turns around slowly, and you see with horror that his face is smeared with blood, and where his shirt opens in the front you can see that his skin is full of cuts and bruises.

"All this suffering," Bythe says, "is going to kill him one day."

Someone in the row in front of you turns around and hisses, "Shh!"

The accused, who is still silent, lifts his bound hands and throws something to the ground. The soil opens up before him. You look closer and see what looks like cornstalks, green and growing upward. You can almost see the plump ears that will soon be ripe for harvest.

But what's this? Between the healthy stalks with plump ears are different plants, growing just as fast but bearing no grain.

Someone from the audience gets up, goes to the front, and says, "Should we pull out the weeds, Lord?"

The accused shakes his head and says, "Both have to grow. If you pull out the weeds, you'll pull out the corn, too, and then they'll both perish. Wait until the harvest."

The judge slams his gavel onto his desk to silence the audience, who have started talking amongst themselves, and cries, "Next, please!"

The blood-smeared accused approaches the judge and says, "I'm next. Give me something to drink!" He looks meaningfully at the glass of water on the judge's desk.

Bythe gets up. "Come on, the show's over."

"But I don't understand what happened," you protest.

Interlude Five

I have to admit, I didn't understand right away either. I know I was just casually talking about how God became human and so forth, but what that really means I can only begin to comprehend. At the very least, it means this: God is suffering from the state of things here. He's not just lazily hanging out in heaven. When he was incarnated as Jesus he got involved in our affairs. He got involved to the point that he was tortured and murdered.

Back in ancient times, that was an unfathomable thought. Downright scandalous. The Greeks—who are known to be wise—took a long time to finally reach the conclusion that if there is a God, and if he is all-powerful, then fundamentally he has to be above and beyond our world. He has to be incapable of suffering!

Why?

Well, the Greeks said that if God suffers, he can't be sovereign anymore. If he lets himself be dragged into human misery, then he can't be a superior, detached ruler anymore. This idea was established long ago. Then the Christians came along, and they claimed that God suffers in Christ. He takes all the suffering upon himself and turns it into glory.

The idea was so out of the blue back then that no one could have just made it up.

This means that when a human being is suffering somewhere on earth, God is passionately taking part in it. And he will compensate them for it.

A famous Christian, the apostle Paul, who had suffered quite a lot himself, writes, "The suffering we are enduring now is nothing compared to the glory we will experience in the future."

As I said, I can't make it any more plausible to you, either. Let me just say this: God really put himself in the defendant's chair and let himself be judged.

Sometimes that comforts me.

SEX IN HEAVEN?

You've grown thoughtful as you and Bythe leave the amphitheater. The two of you walk silently until you reach another park with a huge pond in the middle. There are boats full of people crisscrossing the water, and Bythe says to you, "Let's take a boat. There's still that unspoken question that brought me to you . . ."

Tiny waves of crystal-clear water lap against the shoreline, and you can see every stone and every grain of sand, every silvery fish. Nearby a yellow boat is anchored with two oars.

You can't resist. You take off your sandals and wade around in the clear water. It feels like a foot massage. You notice that here nature always seems to touch something deep inside you. It functions as a kind of felt poetry.

You leave your shoes on the shore and get in the boat. Bythe takes the oars and with a couple of strokes sends you both gliding to the middle of the lake.

A soothing calm comes over you. You can feel the sun's rays piercing right through you, and your heart warms immediately. A thousand little suns are dancing on the waves, and you're surprised you don't need sunglasses.

"Now I remember my question," you say to Bythe. You hesitate a little. It's a touchy subject. You let your hand slip into the cool water and dab your forehead. The water is just glorious. It's as if a stream of cool clarity is flowing through your body.

"You know, Bythe, when we were in hell I noticed that they were having sex there. And when you're in the right mood, that can be pretty nice. In heaven I saw some lovers and . . . well, and seeing that all the men and women here are really attractive . . ."

"And?" Bythe probes. He's a smart guy, seeing that he knows exactly what you want to say. He's like a psychologist on earth who wants you to find your own words to express your problem.

"I imagine that with the body you have here, which feels a thousand times stronger and is a thousand times healthier, your love life could really knock you off your feet."

"Yes, that's true." Bythe nods and then waits, forcing you to continue.

"But I heard somewhere that nothing erotic exists in heaven. That we're going to be somehow genderless. In a film about angels I once saw an angel with absolutely nothing between his legs."

"So this is about sex in heaven, right?"

You nod your head. The wonderful spiritual water is splashing all around you, gurgling and chortling away. It sounds like water music.

"And here in the Foyer?" Bythe asks.

"Here?"

"Yes. This is the afterlife, right? Do you have something between your legs or not?"

"Oh, well—ah—" You're blushing a little. "I haven't actually checked yet."

"Well then, check. I'll turn around for you."

Those angels can be pretty direct, you think, but in the end your curiosity gets the better of you. You open your belt and take a good look. If you are a woman you have probably already noticed that you have quite a nice chest. Not too big, and not too small. And you don't even need a bra.

Once you've checked on everything you say, "You can turn around again."

"So?" Bythe asks and grins.

"Everything's there," you confirm, a bit surprised.

"So now," says Bythe, "the question is if the parts are actually working, right?"

"Geez," you say, "you really cut to the chase."

Bythe starts rowing again while giving you a little lesson about love and sex.

"There is sex in hell and sex in heaven," he begins. "Your body is complete. You have a real heart, real lungs, a real bloodstream, and you can feel your pulse beating just like everything else. But hellish sex is completely different from heavenly sex—just as everything in hell is the exact opposite from what it is in heaven."

Two doves fly over your head and settle on a sunlit rock.

"You've already experienced it," he continues, pulling up one of the oars. "There's no love or affection in hellish sex. Its motive is the domination of others, greed for more. It's a nervous addiction. In the beginning it's a pleasant surprise for the newcomers. Then it becomes mutual torment that you can't live without anymore. And you're never exclusively bound to any one person. Everyone is doing everyone. That might sound like a sexual paradise, but believe me, it's hell."

"And in heaven? Is it only a symbolic act or what?"

Bythe laughs. "You're so skeptical! It's probably because of a particular Bible verse that often gets misinterpreted. In resolving a dispute, Jesus says, 'In heaven there is no marriage. You will be like angels.' People concluded that angels are genderless. But that's nonsense! Marriage doesn't make sense in heaven because two people who belong together will be drawn to each other, if they haven't already found each other on earth. You don't need to sign a paper or fill out a form. In heaven you'll only want to love one person, namely the one you were created for. Man and woman were created together, and it's only when they join as one that they form God's image."

You look around and see people sitting in other boats, some of them lovers. At least two of them are kissing right now.

"So true love really does exist?" you ask tentatively.

"Of course! But it's not always possible to live it out on earth because the emotions are too big; they go beyond the scope of what most people can handle. A marriage needs a certain amount of distance for both partners to endure it. True love is a bleeding into one of two souls. That's difficult for the everyday marriage. But every now and then, it does happen on earth. It very rarely works out. True love was actually made for heaven. This is where it can be lived out. Oh, it's just amazing when you meet the person you've longed for all your life . . ."

You clear your throat as Bythe goes into rapture. Now you know for sure that Bythe used to be an earthly being.

"But to come back to the initial question, Bythe, um, well . . . do the two of them actually have sex in heaven?"

Bythe laughs. "Why don't you just ask the lovers here!"

"What? Just like that?"

"Sure. Come on. I'll row you over."

He grabs the oars and brings you to a blue boat with a couple gazing into each other's eyes, love-struck. The woman is a dark-haired beauty; she is whispering something into the ear of a handsome man who reminds you a little of your sister's violin teacher. Slightly shy, you say hello. Bythe explains briefly what your situation is and that you are very much intrigued with the topic of love. You think that he is exaggerating a bit. You're not really *that* intrigued. Or are you?

"Ask us anything," the woman says and smiles at you. Her smile is charming, welcoming, but nothing even remotely suggestive or sexy.

"How long have you two been together?" you ask.

"Oh," the man says and runs his fingers through his full hair. "A couple of thousand years earthly time, I guess, right?"

"At least," the woman nods.

You are honestly impressed. "And—I don't want to embarrass you—but do you have a sex life here in the Foyer?"

The two of them laugh. "No, no!"

"What? I thought—" You're a little confused now.

"We don't live in the Foyer. We're only here visiting; we live in heaven. But one of our adult children, whom we had lost sight of, is going to be here today, and we're really excited to see him."

"I see." You try again. "So is there sex in heaven?"

"Sex in heaven? No way!" both say in one voice. They seem a little shocked.

"But . . . Bythe told me, and I saw for myself, that we have everything we'd need and that a man and a woman . . ."

"I believe," the man says, "there must be a misunderstanding."

They turn to Bythe, who seems to be having the time of his life. You have a slight suspicion that someone is trying to trick you.

"No, no," Bythe laughs. Of course, he's reading your thoughts again. "Just keep asking."

"So," you try again, feeling like you're on a game show where it's all about finding the right questions. "So, since you're both in love, then I'm sure you hug each other, right?"

"Oh, yes." Both nod their heads and look at each other tenderly.

"And, you kiss . . ."

"That, too."

You had already seen that from further away. "Well, and then after kissing comes sex, right?"

"Oh, that's what you mean," the man says. He pats your back reassuringly. Or, if you're a woman, the other woman would gently stroke your cheek.

"Yes, of course, if both desire so, we unite ourselves with our whole beings," she says. "It's quite exhilarating. But you know, in heaven there isn't any actual sex, only affectionate games. The power of the union is unbelievable, as if an ocean of love is crashing all around you. And it's only possible with the one single person we were created for. It wouldn't even be possible with someone else."

The two of them bow to you politely, and then the man reaches for the oar and the blue boat departs. No one here follows any social rules. If you want to leave, you leave. You watch them, and from a distance it seems as if they are one single person. Once again, you're left with lot to think about.

After a while you ask Bythe, "And you? Where do you stand? Do you have . . ."

"Oh yes. I have a woman I'm connected with day and night. And I will never leave her. That wouldn't be possible anyway, because we have become one person. You remember what the woman said about the great ocean wave!"

"OK. And you're connected to her even now, while we are talking?"

"Even now she's with me, invisibly. And I'm with her. The geographic distance only seems like a distance. We aren't living in the prison of time and space anymore."

"Hm," you say. "I didn't want to be so direct with the others, but I guess I can be with you: Isn't it boring when you're only ever with one person for ever and ever?"

For the first time Bythe gets really angry. His hair sprays sparks and his eyes shoot bolts of lightning. You jump back, terrified, as the boat starts to sway. "Don't you ever say that again!" he cries. "That's an insult to my wife. I just felt her pain inside me when you said that."

But he cools off quickly and puts his hand on your shoulder.

"Don't be afraid. To answer your question, it's actually the opposite. The longer we live, the deeper our affection gets. In true love we find never-ending abundance."

Bythe has rowed the boat back to the shore. You get out, retrieve your shoes, and start walking. It's amazing to walk barefoot. The meadow turns into a series of fields, and you approach a small town, hidden away between two mountains.

Strangely, no matter how long you walk, you don't seem to be getting any closer to the town. You say to Bythe, "Can't we just fly? We don't seem to be making any progress."

"Flying won't help," he says. "Remember when I explained that places and distances only seem to exist here? If you feel uneasy about a place internally, it's expressed in spatial distance."

"So that means that the city over there is giving me a bad feeling?"

"Exactly. You learn quickly. Let's put it this way: You've become estranged from it. In the beginning, when you just arrived, you'd have flown over there like a rocket. But we'll get there eventually."

As you and Bythe continue not to make much progress, you put your shoes back on, and then you remember something. I think I only touched briefly on Christianity and church in the park scene. I have something to catch up on. But if you're not interested, you can just continue in the next chapter.

Interlude Six

The thing about Christianity and the church is this: I know a lot of people who say to me, "I left the church because they're just a bunch of arrogant hypocrites. Christians think they're better than everyone else. And the services just bore me to death."

What am I supposed to say to that? I am a Christian myself, so I'm a member of that club. Some of the criticism I can understand, but not everything.

I'm sure there are Christians who are self-righteous and arrogant. And there are churches that make you want to fall asleep. But I always say to myself: the fact that there are a couple of bad bakeries doesn't mean that all baguettes have to be bad.

I personally know of churches where you feel comfortable. Places where, when you're there, it seems a lot easier to love God and your neighbor. That's what the original idea was. Then, when the Christian church was made the official state religion of the Roman Empire, it got too involved with power and politics. It wasn't very becoming to the church. It evolved into this huge, bureaucratic apparatus of power, responsible for killing and persecuting innocent people. Luckily, that has stopped now.

But still it's important that there is a church. Christian rituals have something positive and beautiful. The Lord's Supper, for example, is just amazing—God's presence is particularly close, almost tangible. A church service can lift up your soul, and through a good interpretation of the Bible, God can often explain concepts that you otherwise would never have understood.

I personally love church music and sing in a choir. It's wonderful. No doubt about it.

But whether or not you get into heaven doesn't depend first and foremost on your church membership. I hope you've got that by now. And you have to keep one thing in mind: All those many Christian rules and rituals, the sometimes strict distinction between believers and nonbelievers, all of that will disappear after death anyway, because those were only crutches some people needed for their faith to grow. Like a young tree that is bound to a wooden stick so the wind won't blow it over. So please be patient with Christians. They're on a journey as well.

And by the way, did you know that one of the first names for Christians was "the ones on their way"?

Maybe you will decide to become a Christian after this story has finished. And why shouldn't you? You only have to accept that the church is never perfect and that it's very human. In the end, it's made up of humans. Here on earth, perfection feels sterile, like some distant, unreal utopia.

So, if you manage to stay humble as a Christian, you'll have a pretty good chance of getting into heaven. As a Christian, you believe that God became human, that he cleared the way for you to enter heaven because he took upon himself anything that could come between you and God. And as a Christian you'll experience the love of God.

When you're in church, you're normally encouraged to turn to God again and again and to put your love into action. Those are also the prerequisites for getting into heaven.

But there's one more thing I'd like to ask of you: Should you wish to become a Christian, then please be careful not to be self-righteous and arrogant and look down on the non-Christians. Otherwise you'll need a remedial course to keep you out of hell. And I'd like to help you avoid that one.

All right, then, by now you've reached the city after a long but steady march, and I'm anxious to see what awaits you. ⚘

CITY OF THE UNTEACHABLES

If you didn't know this was the afterlife, you'd swear you were now approaching your typical European or American town. In the town center you see older houses, on the outskirts are more modern apartment buildings, and beyond that are single-family homes with gardens. You see streets full of cars and bikes, mothers and fathers with baby carriages, shops . . . everything you'd expect to see in a town on earth.

"What is this?" you might ask Bythe.

"Oh, that's the city of the Unteachables."

This sounds interesting, and you remember one of your grandmother's friends mentioning a city. You ask again, and Bythe explains that this is the place for those people who only believed what they could see with their eyes and touch with their hands. They rejected the idea of a life after death, calling it nothing more than escapism. One has to be realistic about these kinds of things, they said. To them, the spiritual realm was just the evaporation from our glands, a chemical reaction in our brain. And they believed that when you die, you're completely dead, like a tree that's cut down and rots on the ground. After death, they said, you only live in the memories of your loved ones. This phrase would come to be repeated mindlessly in countless obituaries.

But you already know that. Basically, it's just a more modern take on Mr. Feuerbach's ideas. If you skipped the first interlude, this might be a good moment to catch up on the Feuerbach story. But only if you're interested, of course.

Anyway, you laugh involuntarily as a realization hits you. "Oh, now I understand why the city was so far away. My horizon has already broadened through our conversations and experiences."

"That's right," Bythe confirms. "You're not quite as bullheaded as the people here anymore!"

"But Bythe," you say, "why are they still so stubborn? They're here now. Isn't that proof enough of an afterlife?"

Bythe shakes his head. "If a person believed in something strongly enough for many years, that can be pretty tough. Their belief was fed over and over again with many arguments. It's like a red wine stain—it's hard to get out. People cling to their cherished beliefs, even if you prove the opposite. That's why you shouldn't rely on getting your act together after you've died. If people don't manage to change their thinking here, they'll end up in hell sooner or later. As long as you live on earth, it's easier to change your mind. You aren't quite as locked in to a particular way of thinking as you are in the Foyer, and you've got more freedom."

What Bythe is saying seems rather odd to you. Unable to believe what he's telling you, you ask, "Can I talk to these people myself?"

"Sure, go ahead."

"And the houses, the cars, the shops—they're all real?"

"Well," Bythe says, "what is real? The only real thing is someone's inner life. What you are manifests itself as something solid. Just think about the gloomy atmosphere in hell, or the light, intense environment in heaven. In the minds of these people there is no other dimension, so they're living in the one environment they can believe in. The houses are solid and the cars really drive around. Matter here is more perfect and more versatile than on earth. But please, go ahead and ask them yourself!"

That's exactly what you want to do. *It'd be ridiculous,* you think, *if these city-dwellers couldn't be convinced of the fact that they're living in the afterlife!*

Bythe says goodbye and leaves you to the Unteachables. But you don't really mind, since you're feeling somewhat superior— and if you feel superior, you aren't afraid.

You go to an outdoor café and ask a young couple if you may sit at their table. You may. And the friendly waiter comes right away, smiles at you warmly, and takes your order. You ask for coffee and apple strudel with cream. Good thing you don't have to worry about calories anymore.

"You know, I'm not from this area," you begin. "Have you been living here long?"

The two of them exchange glances, and the woman says, "We've only been here for about three years and—"

"I'm sorry, honey, but hasn't it been five years?"

She looks at her companion. "That's strange. It seems a lot shorter to me."

"It doesn't really matter, I guess," you say. You already know what you want to ask next. "Where did you live before?"

The woman is silent. Finally, she says, "Are you going to move here?"

"No!" You shake your head. "I'm just passing through."

She looks at her companion tellingly—you assume he's her husband—then she lowers her voice and whispers, "Where we used to live . . . it's kind of a strange thing."

"Why?" you ask. Maybe you're already beginning to suspect what the woman is talking about. You try to look at the other tables unobtrusively. She continues, "I guess I can tell you. Since you're not going to live here and will be leaving soon, there's no risk for us. The thing is: Fred and I can't remember the move. We used to live in Hamburg, and now we're here. Everything is great. I don't want to complain. We've both found work, the climate is pleasant. The cost of living is OK . . . but . . . why have we ended up in this small town? I don't understand it!"

"Um—" You try to be helpful. "What do the others say? How are they handling it?"

Fred bursts out laughing. "We know better than to tell everyone about our memory lapse. Imagine you meet someone new who tells you, 'I don't even know how I got here.' You'd think the guy's not all there. I . . ." Fred seems a little shocked as he continues, "I'm still surprised that Tanya told you in the first place. It's always been our secret."

Tanya looks at the floor, embarrassed, and whispers, "It was such a relief to meet someone who's going somewhere else, to just tell at least one person that we're not . . ." She looks at you pleadingly and asks, "You really are going to leave this town again, aren't you?"

You start to feel sorry for the two of them and assure them a second time that you're just passing through. That seems to comfort them a lot. And it's true! Now you feel the moment has come to give them a hint. You also lower your voice and say, "You know something—"

But then you are interrupted by the coffee and apple strudel's seductive aroma as the waiter sets them in front of you. You take a quick bite and close your eyes before this poem of a pastry. Then you wait for the waiter—who seems to be eyeing you suspiciously—to disappear.

You drink a sip of your delicious coffee and make a second attempt. "You know, I think I might know why you're having this problem."

"What do you mean?" the man whispers back.

"I think I know why you can't remember ever moving here. There's a simple explanation for it."

Fred and Tanya look at each other, interested. "We're all ears," Fred says.

"What I'm going to tell you now . . ." You pause, searching for the right words. "Well, um, it might sound totally crazy, but hear me out first."

"We're listening!"

"It's possible," you say slowly and carefully, "that you both have died and are now in the afterlife. Do you understand? In a transitional realm that's between heaven and hell. That's why you can't remember moving here. It was probably an accident or—"

The man smiles. "You mean, we're ghosts?"

You scratch your head. "Well, ghost might not be the right word. Let's say you're living in a spiritual kind of world. Your earthly body is lying in a grave somewhere on earth while you are . . . Do you by any chance remember traveling by car or plane right before the end?"

"This is outrageous!" Tanya bursts in. "Just because we can't remember moving, you come along with this nonsense!"

Fred says, "I don't know what's happening here, but about a year ago someone else was here and told us the same crazy thing.

Listen! We are sitting on metal chairs, drinking coffee with our solid bodies, wearing normal clothes, and then you show up and tell us we're ghosts! There are no ghosts! There is no life after death! We only believe in what we can see and touch! Come on, Tanya, let's get out of here!" The two stand up and go up to the waiter, pay their bill, and disappear into one of the side streets.

All of a sudden the waiter is at your side, not looking so friendly anymore, asking, "You want your bill?" The way he says it leaves no doubt about what he actually wanted to say: "Just pay your bill, get lost, and don't bother any of my guests again!" Somewhat taken aback, you reach into your pocket and find some of the silver coins. You put them on the table and hurry out of the café.

OK, you think to yourself. *The first attempt failed.* You take a stroll along the river and think about how the apparently serene city is not so serene after all, because all of the people have the same problem: No one can remember moving here, and they're all desperate to keep that secret from the others. *That'd kill me eventually*, you think. And you're right. That'd kill me, too.

In the afternoon, you try having some more conversations. You sit in the waiting room of a hospital, but find that you're just banging your head against the wall when you try to suggest that the people waiting are actually already dead. You go into a bar and narrowly avoid a fight. Only as the daylight starts to fade you do finally meet a man who is standing on a bridge, pensively feeding the ducks. He seems to be the only one willing to at least consider your idea, and thanks you before saying goodbye. ⚘

EVENING GLORY

Still quite disillusioned about the stubbornness of the residents of the city of the Unteachables, you wander on. After a while, you've left the center of the city and are now passing some single-family homes. A certain melancholy takes hold of you as you notice the afternoon sun slowly dimming into a softer evening light, the blue of the sky above you turning pale.

You keep thinking about your experiences in the city, how certain people aren't able to see the truth because it doesn't fit their old worldview, and for the first time you have to accept that arguments alone won't persuade another person. You kind of knew that before, but now it's become particularly clear.

From one of the houses you hear an instrument that sounds like a saxophone playing a low, solemn melody. The composition flows beautifully. It vibrates with intensity. But the chords underlying the melody aren't like anything you heard on earth, even though the similarities are there. It's like someone added overtones unknown to the terrestrial ear, blurring the lines between classical music and jazz. It might be the sort of blues improvised by Händel had he lived three hundred years longer. Suddenly, you realize that you are hearing exactly the music you want to hear. Someone from another cultural background would probably hear a different type of music.

Then you notice something strange. Just a little while ago, you thought that the sun was setting, but if you look into the far distance, you see that the sun is still shining brightly in other areas. However, the closer you get to the house the music is coming from, the darker it gets. Someone has switched on the lights outside the house. Intrigued, you move closer.

As you stroll through an alley lined with roses, the wind rustles the leaves, and the difference becomes more and more apparent: the house itself is surrounded by an evening light. A small lake mirrors the lights of multicolored paper lanterns. Giant trees have retreated into the dark of night while the remaining surroundings are in bright daylight.

You once saw a picture very much like this in a book of paintings by René Magritte; the painting you're thinking of was called *Empire of Light*. The landscape is in daylight, but the house is in darkness.

And then, luckily, you remember what Bythe told you earlier in your journey: In the otherworld, the inner state of things, including their emotions, will find appropriate outward forms.

You go through the gate, and it's like passing from midday to evening. When you look upward, you see a beautiful night sky complete with gloriously sparkling stars, like a blanket full of diamonds. But as soon as you turn away from the house and the music, you see a sunny summer landscape in the distance.

It's exhilarating. You wish you could take a picture. The atmosphere feels like the calm before a thunderstorm: on one side of the sky the sun is shining and on the other side dark clouds are brewing.

The music gets louder and becomes so expressive that you choke up with emotion. You walk along a gravel path, look through one of the windows, and see a group of musicians playing their brass instruments—but so soft and gentle—it's almost too perfect. Two men are crying while they play. It's somehow beautiful.

One of the musicians, a woman with something resembling a trombone, lowers her instrument and looks up at you, smiling.

"Come in," she says, and waves her hand to show you where to find the door. You follow her directions and enter a cultivated garden smelling of ripe tomatoes. You see the open patio door.

The living room looks homey. There's no other word for it: it has comfortable soft chairs, a table with filled wine glasses and snacks, and pictures on the wall whose images move in time with the music.

One of the crying men takes a break. He holds his hand under his eyes, collects his tears, and lifts them up in the air, where they evaporate. A delicate mist floats from his hand out of the window.

You let yourself sink into one of the soft chairs and listen to the music, which is just ending on a full chord.

Of course, you start clapping your hands. The artists jokingly take a bow and the trombone player hands you a glass of wine.

"What brings you to this neighborhood?" asks one of the men, who is holding an instrument like a French horn.

"Well, I'm kind of passing through and taking a look around . . . and . . . then I heard your music."

"Oh, so you're one of the near-death wanderers?"

"No, my body's not in a hospital. I'm actually a fictitious character from a book."

"I see." The woman nods. "Yes, that happens from time to time. A certain Lewis once showed up here, too, and I heard about this Italian guy who wrote a huge poem about it."

Her kindness makes you brave enough to ask the question that's been on your mind since you first heard the music. "It seems to me like you're sad . . ."

"Yes," the man with the French horn says, "we've come from heaven and have visited some friends in the city of the Unteachables. They recognized us and were happy to see us, but they didn't want to believe they were dead. We talked until we could talk no more. No chance. We were afraid that our friends would eventually end up in hell if they didn't change their direction. That's what put us in this mood and brought dusk over the house."

"Hm," you say, your mind working. "I thought once you were close to heaven, in this paradise, you wouldn't be sad anymore."

"Well," the woman says, taking a sip of her wine, "there's a good kind of sorrow and a bad kind. The good kind of sorrow makes our hearts better. We cry and hold our tears up to God."

"I see," you say. "But in heaven you don't cry anymore, right?"

"Of course we do! What did you think? We cry even more than before, because our hearts have become a lot softer, and eventually we have to let out all those pent-up tears. But it's a good, soothing kind of sadness, releasing new energy. After all, it's said that God will wipe away all of our tears. So there have to be tears. The crying and comforting in heaven is an experience you wouldn't want anyone to miss out on. The kind of joy that comes after mourning is twice as beautiful, almost overwhelming."

You feel very much at home with these sad-happy people, as if you could stay here for days. A place where it's OK to cry without shame is something quite beautiful.

Just when you're about to ask more about heaven, a door next to you opens and Bythe comes strolling in. He gives the group a friendly nod and says, "The time is just right." He hands you a white cloak with a white hat. "The moment has come. We can spend some time in heaven now." 🌱♡🌱

FLYING TOUR OF HEAVEN

You say goodbye to the sad-happy people and follow Bythe outside into a different time of day. On the way, you put on your cloak, which is light as a feather on your skin and not even the slightest bit scratchy. A truly precious material. When you put on the hat, it seems like someone just dimmed the lights.

Once again, you are standing in front of the mother of all doors. It opens and you enter for the second time. But the landscape around you has somehow changed. Everything here seems to be in flux.

Again you feel your skin tingle, though not quite as strongly as last time, and you breathe in the unbelievable freshness that made you feel so drunk before.

A slight sense of fear takes hold of you when you think of your life on earth, but it's just enough that you can still take it.

"That's because you haven't had your Great Examination yet," says Bythe good-humoredly. Of course he can still hear your thoughts.

"What examination?"

"You mean you've never heard of it? Judgment Day."

"Oh, sh—" You can just barely hold yourself back.

"Call it what you like. You can also say harvest."

Involuntarily, you think about the field of corn in the amphitheater and remember Bythe telling you that the time spent in the Foyer is a sort of process of separation. Because the corn has to be separated from the weeds. Right.

"When you've completed the examination like your grandmother," Bythe explains, "meaning when you've become more like yourself, then you'll feel better. You'll be able to better understand your life, and you'll have time to repent a couple of things and rethink others. Then the atmosphere in heaven will revive rather than drain you."

"And when is that going to happen for me?"

"Should I remind you that you haven't actually died yet? You're just a character in a story."

"Oh, right."

"That's why you need the cloak. You wouldn't even be able to tolerate it here without a prior life examination."

"Exactly."

You're walking along a lane lined by ancient, massive trees. A solemn feeling comes over you. Something like awe. You hear steps behind you and turn around. A young man has followed and caught up to you. The serious expression on his face frightens you a little. But when he smiles at you and stretches out his hand, it's as if the sun is rising.

"Welcome," he says. "Are you visiting here?"

You nod, reassured by his warm greeting.

"I can tell by your safety cloak." He winks at Bythe knowingly, and Bythe winks back, grinning. The two seem to know each other.

"And how do you like it here?" the man asks. You would love to know his name, but are too timid to ask. Maybe he's one of the celebrities here who prefers to remain incognito.

"Oh, I actually like it a lot," you say, "but . . . but I have to admit I felt even more at home in the Foyer."

"Of course you did," he says, and you can feel his compassion like a warm wave in your belly. *Politeness doesn't seem to exist here, only genuine emotion,* you think.

"That's the reason why you don't feel quite at home here yet," says the stranger, who knows your thoughts. "Living completely truthfully needs some getting used to, and you haven't been properly prepared for heaven. But let me tell you, once you have been prepared you won't ever want to leave again." He shakes your hand and says, "Take care! I hope we'll meet again."

You are overwhelmed by his handshake. A sense of heaven's glory is flooding through you, making your skin tingle pleasantly. If you were a cat, you'd likely start to purr.

Then, all of a sudden, he's gone.

"So who was that?" you ask. "I didn't dare ask him. Was that another angel, one of your colleagues, or Francis of Assisi?"

Bythe pats you on the back amiably and says, "That was God."

You stop dead. "What? That was . . . but I always thought . . ."

Bythe explains, "Your grandmother told you in the park that we can never truly meet God because he's so great. If you actually stood in his presence, you'd melt like snow in the sun. If you could hear God's voice directly, your ears would burst. That's what the ant story was all about. But God has a human form he can use to come face-to-face with us. He even spent a few years on earth, with all the ups and downs of a mortal existence. Quite a bloody story, actually. He knows what he's talking about. His spirit pulsates through everything here."

"Oh, I get it," you say. "That's the Trinity again, isn't it? It's not actually three separate gods, but only one God in three different forms of appearance?"

"That's exactly it. Like the sun: heat, light, and sunbeams. Three, but one sun, you know. Most Christians in the second century still believed in multiple gods until the Roman emperor changed the state religion."

"In any case," you say, "it was quite an experience to meet God. I'll never forget that."

"And now imagine having met him without your safety cloak. I probably would have had to carry you out again."

While you were talking, you entered a big city. Wonderful aromas are everywhere. You hear the sound of a violin that is so captivating and uplifting you start to dance and cry for joy.

Bythe takes a snow-white handkerchief from his pocket and dries your tears, because you aren't able to anymore. Your hands are shaking with excitement.

"Heaven," you cry, and spin around and around while new tears drop to the floor. "Is it just this endless feast?"

Bythe laughs and shakes his head emphatically. "Are you crazy? Come on, let's walk a little further, or you'll really lose your mind."

He guides you away from the music so you have a chance to calm down. Then he explains, "Heaven is not just the land of milk and honey. You'd get tired of that after a while. An eternal feast would eventually bore everyone to death. We humans and angels aren't built to tolerate unending joy. We need some work every once in a while. We need to create and do something that helps us advance and is useful to others. Then we're ready to celebrate again! Come here, I'll show you something!"

Then he takes your hand and you fly with him across the city, buzzing with life and cheerful ruckus.

You stop on one of the rooftops and look down at the streets. They're filled with people and animals who all seem to be moving with a purpose. In between you see beautifully designed plazas with benches where people are sitting and chatting.

"Everyone here has something to do," Bythe says. "And when the work is done, it's truly done."

"Wait a minute. What do people in heaven have to do? Everything is already perfect here!"

"No, no," Bythe says. "Everything is only in the process of becoming perfect, and thank God for that. There are schools and universities to further your education. There are teachers, of course, and craftsmen who make many beautiful things, architects, cooks, caretakers of the humans on earth. You call them guardian angels. You know, earth is only one planet among many that have people. Here in heaven we have buildings where new inventions are being planned and then later sent to earth. There are weaving mills where human fates are been interwoven with each other. There are kindergartens for the many children here who died too early. We have regular meetings of women who arrange marriages on earth. There are the most wonderful services. There are so many things here, really."

In spite of your safety cloak you start to feel a bit anxious trying to process all your impressions, and you ask Bythe to take you somewhere a little quieter.

You fly further until you get to a park with a fountain. But Bythe passes right by the fountain and lands in a giant tree. You are reminded of your childhood, when you and your friends used to climb all sorts of trees together.

A hammock is extended between two big branches.

"Lie down here," Bythe says, "and relax a little!"

It's glorious to be lying in the hammock. You start to relax, listening to the rustling of the leaves, and then you hear a peculiar, gripping series of musical notes. It almost seems like the tree is humming a song.

You start getting sleepy. Your eyes get heavy and you drift into unconsciousness.

When you wake up again, you feel refreshed. It seems as if you've only slept a second—or three hundred years. There's no opposition between the two here. Time conforms to your awareness.

You spend a little while just watching the sunbeams playing with the leaves. When you get up from the hammock, you see a play of lights far above you in the sky, like sheet lightning before a thunderstorm.

"What's that?" you ask Bythe, pointing upward.

Bythe, who had been talking to a child, turns around and says, "That's the next heaven. From here all you can see are flashes of light every now and then, a bit of heaven's glory seeping through to us."

"What?" You're perplexed. "There's another heaven?"

"Of course. This is only the lowest one. There are at least three heavens, if not more. Maybe even seven. Heaven's heavens."

"And what's happening up there?"

"The glory up there is so tremendous, you'd melt from happiness."

"You think we could at least get a glimpse?"

"Hm." Bythe slowly shakes his head. "That's only possible with an even heavier cloak. I'll see what I can do."

HEAVEN'S HEAVEN

The robe you're putting on now is much thicker and heavier, and the hat seems to swallow every ray of light. *The first heaven is just hitting twilight,* you think. But that's only an illusion caused by your safety clothes.

Bythe takes your hand, and the two of you fly up in the air, closer and closer to the sheet lightning.

Then you're standing in front of a door that is even more impressive than the mother of all doors. Maybe it should be called the grandmother of all doors.

A giant angel resembling a lion with a human face cries, "Stop!" so loudly that you almost lose your sense of hearing. It's what we would call a cherub. Frightening and glorious all at once.

Even Bythe has difficulty looking at the angel as he whispers something into his ear. The cherub takes a step aside and opens the door a tiny bit.

Bythe gestures with his hand, whispering, "Just a little glimpse."

With a pounding heart you step closer and carefully lean forward. Then you freeze. Something like a white horse is galloping toward you, and the rider's face is radiating a joy so intense that anything else that has made you joyful and happy before would collapse back onto itself in comparison. You would feel burned out and empty next to it.

In fact, you feel as if you're burning right now. With a final effort, you throw your whole body weight against the door to shut it.

You remain in front of the door, numb and gasping for air.

Bythe, who has a good sense about these things, hands you a cup with some liquid in it. "Drink!" he orders you.

You drink. It tastes delicious.

"What is this?"

"It's a beverage that will help you forget your sight of pure joy; otherwise you wouldn't ever be able to get happy again. Now you'll only have an intuition that the joy in heaven can never be fully exhausted."

Bythe helps you stand up again, supporting you so that you don't fall. He nods to the cherub, and you and Bythe float back down to a street in the first heaven.

You feel like someone who has just been released from the hospital and has to slowly relearn how to walk, just like you did on your first visit to heaven.

"Wow," you whisper. "How can anyone live there?"

"Oh, it's quite easy. A lot of human beings and angels live there. But you need time to grow accustomed to the new level of vitality." ⚘

THE RETURN

The street you slowly continue to walk down takes you directly to the door of heaven, as if the distance had been shortened especially for you—which is actually exactly what happened.

Again you are standing outside looking at the park-like landscape of the Foyer, which has almost become a second home to you.

In front of you, two wolves are singing a song. When you look closer, you see that they are actually two sheep in wolves' clothing.

Bythe, seeing your surprise, laughs. "They're practicing for a comedy show."

Someone is playing a grand piano accompanying the two innocent wolves.

"Later there will be a performance in the big tent for the people who've woken up. After their long processing time, they need something to make them laugh."

"And can I go there too?" you ask Bythe.

"I don't think so," he says gently, patting you on the back.

"Why not?"

"Well, dear friend," he tells you, "the time has come for you to return to earth again. I hope you now know what's in store for you. It's up to you to decide how you want to live your life now."

"Stop!" you cry, because this is starting to sound like goodbye. "So much has happened. What do I have to do to know if I want to get into heaven later?"

"I told you that when you first came here. You have to be renewed inwardly, or reborn, if you later want to be able to handle the glories of heaven. You have to have heaven inside of you in order to enjoy the heaven outside."

"Yeah, yeah, but . . . where do I start? Do I have to go back into a woman's body to be born again?"

Bythe shakes his head. "No, no. I'll try to make it practical for you: Find yourself a quiet room when you're back home again and pray to God in your own words. Tell him you want to live with him and accept his love. It's totally free, you know. You can't buy it and you can't earn it. Then take a piece of paper and write down everything you did wrong in your life. Ask God for forgiveness. That's a good start. And try, as best as you can, to love God and your neighbor. If you can't do it on your own, find some other Christians you can rely on and meet with them every now and then. You can also go to a church."

With that, he gives you a gentle kick. You stumble forward, fall over, and slowly roll down a hill ending in a placid valley.

Above you—or is it next to you?—you can still hear Bythe's voice calling out, "And I'll be around too, watching over you, even though you won't see me!"

You finally come to a stop on the grass. You look to the side and notice the meadow is a carpet. When you get up and turn around, you are in your living room in front of the bookshelf. A book with a mysterious-looking cover attracts your attention. You take it out. The title is *Getting into Heaven,* and below that you read *—and Out Again!*

You say to yourself, "OK, so now I've gotten to the subtitle. I hope this isn't where it ends."

I hope so too. See you later—in heaven. 🌣

EPILOGUE

That was quite an adventure, wasn't it? It really got me thinking . . . how much more can we learn about the afterlife? What if we could spend some more time with the people who live there?

Well, it turns out that we can. I used my—authorial influence, let's say—to arrange some interviews. One is with a certain individual named Mephistopheles; another gives Bythe a little more air time; and then we will have an interview in which the protagonist, the *fictional* reader, gets to talk about how the journey into the Beyond has changed his life.

Let's start with the interview with Mephistopheles. Please don't ask how this came about. It was difficult enough as it was. Our scheduled appointments were canceled at the last minute, and Mr. M. was in a bad mood or generally irritable. But in the end, we finally met up.

Mephistopheles

AG: Mr. M., our readers probably know you from Faust. Thinking about you always conjures up an image of a pale face and diabolic grin. You've become somewhat of a cult figure. Writers like Thomas Mann dedicated whole chapters to you, with a freezing sort of charm. What I would like to do today is talk about your self-conception and about your home. So, hell—the place of evil—

M: Be careful with that word. My roommates and I don't really see ourselves as evil. This term was ascribed to us from the other side. We would rather describe our lifestyle as freedom from the yoke of having to be good all the time.

AG: Or the pressure of having to condemn everything good.

M: Very funny.

AG: Maybe we can come back to that later. What our readers are interested in is, for example, the geography of hell. Where exactly is it located? Thanks to you we finally have a reliable source. As you are probably aware, there have been the most fantastic theories about the location of hell. One is that it is situated at the center of the earth. Many of us know the novel by Jules Verne, *A Journey to the Center of the Earth*. In the nineteenth century, people thought there were different spheres of hell, accommodating entire civilizations. Some people imagine the entrance to the center of the earth at the polar ice caps. And in the Middle Ages some scholars located the inhabitants of hell inside the sun, in a great hot hollow . . .

M: Enough already! That's ridiculous. You're on the wrong track entirely. I'm the spirit who negates; I have nothing to do with the sun's fire or earthly mire, with rocks, deep drilling or any of those other notions. Take a good look: Do I have dirt under my nails?

AG: Let me see . . . You're right—your nails are surprisingly well manicured. Then this hell thing is just an illusion, a figment of our imagination? And when the reader was in the Foyer just now, it wasn't actually the afterlife at all?

M: What nerve! Of course I exist. I hate, therefore I am. Hell exists, too. But you'll have to rid yourself of some stupid ideas, like hell existing in a specific location. Hell is a spiritual world. You saw that in your previous excursions. That doesn't mean it's insubstantial. Within the spiritual world all things are tangible, but we have a very different type of matter: spiritual matter.

AG: But where exactly can this spiritual hell, this gigantic space you're talking about, be found?

M: Good devil, you don't know anything, do you? Spiritual matter is independent of space and time. Hell can exist right in the center of Berlin or New York while you're walking down the street, shopping or going about your business. Just like that so-called heaven could exist anywhere. Above and below refer to conditions in this world; they don't apply to heaven and hell in a geographical way. If your spiritual senses were completely open, you would be able to look down into abysses right here, in front of your feet, because spiritual perception is stronger than physical perception. You'd be able to see angels and smell their disgusting natural scent, or taste the intense flavors of hell.

AG: So you smell and feel, too?

M: Of course, you imbecile.

AG: You feel joy as well as pain?

M: Certainly. Pain suits us. As far as joy goes, I'm afraid I can only offer some malicious pleasure in others' misery.

AG: Who would have thought that hell is right here, among us? I always assumed you had to travel far or die first to see it.

M: Oh, come on. Are you telling me your contemporaries seriously only believe in a three-dimensional world and don't let their imaginations go beyond that? That's so backward! You should really allow your mind to explore a spiritual universe, especially since it's just a hand's-width away. There are many worlds, you know. Death is only a door, another birth canal. Hell starts inside you and becomes your reality in the spiritual world. I bet that most human beings have already had a foretaste of hell at times . . .

AG: And a foretaste of heaven!

M: Yeah, yeah. That, too.

AG: What about all the torment in hell? I caught at least a little glimpse of that. Despicable.

M: Torment! Again the wrong word in the wrong context! Whenever I accidently stray into heaven on a matter of business—which happens very rarely—I can never stand it for very long. That atmosphere is what I call torment. I have trouble breathing. And then there's this unpleasant smell in the air. It's not a coincidence that the prologue in Faust is rather short.

AG: Still, you're quoted as saying, "I like to hear the Old Man's words, from time to time."

M: Oh, please! Mr. Goethe put words into my mouth. For me, heaven is hell! The contact with that form of undiluted goodness is sickening. And if I may refer back to something I said before, I would like to add that hell definitely evokes positive associations in me: unfathomable depth, pleasant darkness, protection from—

AG: —from heavenly light!

M: Naturally we have to protect ourselves from the ever-present openness and transparency in heaven, you know, all that shining and gleaming, that . . . that terrible brilliance and vastness. For someone like me, that's hard to bear. Thank badness for the hellish safe rooms!

AG: But isn't it also freeing not to have to hide anymore? I find it awful being on guard all the time. Isn't there any real kind of openness in hell?

M: Oh, for hell's sake! That sounds awful to me. What about privacy? Not everything is for everyone to know.

AG: Privacy in hell? That almost sounds cozy. Don't tell me you all sit around the campfire, sing songs, and roast marshmallows!

M: No! No! No idyllic moments! In hell, we're all truly wicked. I even love that word. I really do.

AG: Atta boy.

M: In hell we all fight against one another, we try to outdo each other, we bathe in hatred and contempt. The word love exists only in the context of narcissism. We love only one person: ourselves. But radically. We make each other's lives hell.

AG: "The Devil is an egoist / Does nothing lightly, or in God's name / To help another."

M: You said it. This time the prince of poets was completely right; this is the source of our life. It's the fuel of our hellish fire. There's no fussy, sappy harmony. Just hearing the word makes me sick. We have hearts of stone and need the fire to warm them at least a little. We find pleasure in mutual torture—

AG: Torture that hurts.

M: Granted. But still, a torture we desire, even though we also detest it. That's why we need hell with all its bunkers, houses, and caves, in order to shield us from the harmony-addicted influence of heaven, which is far too bright for us.

AG: There we have it again: Hell as a place of protection from light.

M: Protection from light! You make it sound so wrong. It's not like I don't like light, just make it the dimmed kind. The light from heaven is unspeakably unpleasant. It must be of a very inferior quality. It irritates and stings like salt in a wound. In comparison, our own hellish atmosphere is wonderful: We destroy each other. There's combat and struggle, and we hurt each other, and there's no recreation. We suffer without relief. We love to set a snare and gloat when others fall into it. We're always seeking the latest perversions. We wallow in the dirt. We would kill each other if we weren't dead already. And I invite everyone who enjoys this to spend the rest of their lives in hell. That's what keeps us alive, after all. And if you don't get that, you're naïve. In my home, there's never a dull moment.

AG: Sure. All hell is allowed to break loose.

M: And listen what the Old Man above says himself:

> Man's energies all too soon seek the level,
> He quickly desires unbroken slumber,
> So I gave him to you to join the number,
> To move, and work, and pass for the devil.

AG: That's not exactly flattering for you.

M: Why?

AG: Well, because it sounds like you and your colleagues still have to serve God. Kind of like God's fleas, biting us to remind us that we need to have a wash from time to time . . .

M: Are you trying to insult me? Go ahead. This conversation is way too dull and innocent for me anyway. I'd love to see you lash out at me with some hatred.

AG: That'll be difficult, seeing that I'm so naïve. I'm afraid I just don't see the appeal of your devilish values. And you're lying when you say that you actually enjoy all the torture. It sounds more like cheap propaganda. For my part, I love the vastness of a natural landscape or the splendor of the sun reflecting on the ocean. I love getting close to someone, opening up and losing myself. My heart starts racing when I hear the *Magnificat* by Bach, the *Violin Concerto in D Major* by Brahms, or Van Morrison's "You Steal My Heart Away." Your description of hell leaves me cold. I don't want to have to crawl into a hole like a worm who's afraid of the light.

M: Well, well! Let's be honest here. You can't make me believe you don't want to dive into the subterranean perversions of hell. Have you never gloated over the failures of a person you deeply disliked? Did you never feel the desire to kill him or her? Have you never smothered your bitterness like a little baby or worn your grudges like armor? Have you never felt like having a rowdy orgy or embracing the rush of destruction?

AG: I admit, some of these things hold a certain attraction. I've fallen for them and will probably fall for them again. But I can tell you one thing: Don't believe that evil has a monopoly on excitement. God knows people like Martin Luther King Jr., Astrid Lindgren, Francis of Assisi, and Joan of Arc didn't lead boring lives. Their lives were full of vim and vigor. Don't give me that tired cliché about evil being exciting and good being boring. What nonsense! The front yards of the houses with the really evil parties are full of vomit the next morning.

When I imagine all of that happening underground, with no fresh air, I can just about smell the disgusting stench you must live in—and no one ever opens a window.

M: Look at you! You're really on a roll. But don't worry, sooner or later we're all pulled into the current that takes us to my kingdom. There is no real change. You may be able to hide the predator inside you, but you will never extinguish it.

All you need is a small catastrophe and your veneer of Western education falls off, and your greed bursts out and grasps for more. How did Faust put it so wonderfully?

> In the end, you are—what you are.
> Set your hair in a thousand curlicues,
> Place your feet in yard-high shoes,
> You'll remain forever, what you are.

AG: Ah, I see. So that's your secret creed, Mr. M.—and I agree with you for once!

M: What? I must have misheard! You agree with me that a person cannot truly change?

AG: Of course he can't. The urge to only love oneself and no one else is strong. A person can only forget himself once he has encountered the great love of the Maker. You can't pull yourself out of the mess.

M: Damn! You're right! It's the reason quite a few have slipped through our fingers. There's only one comfort.

AG: Oh?

M: People have to want to change of their own free will. The Master upstairs loves freedom, that childish gift of his! And many people tend to prefer sticking to their tired old ways rather than choosing to love their neighbors voluntarily, accept hardships, and entertain a relationship with an invisible God. Everyone thinks their own sweat smells the best.

AG: Really? So you've never been in love, then?

M: That must be the stupidest type of relationship there is.

AG: That's one way to see it, of course. And by the way, God is not invisible.

M: Oh, did I miss something?

AG: There's an incarnation of God in Christm—

M: *(Screaming)* Don't you dare say that despicable word! We've been working hard to revamp that horrific feast, trying to add unnecessary hustle and bustle, increasing the expectations for unrealistic harmony to the point that fighting becomes inevitable.

AG: But that still leaves one of the biggest attractions of heaven: beauty!

M: Beauty? That's all just appearances. We also offer a certain kind of beauty: the beauty of the monstrous, the ugly. That's far more impressive, you know. In hell we can show you some real monsters, the kind that give you serious goose bumps. Your horror films are like valium in comparison.

AG: I'm talking about beauty that lifts you up inside. You can only find that kind in heaven, where you can step outside and walk, awestruck, across a meadow filled with wildflowers and fluttering butterflies, ringed by breathtaking mountain ranges. Where there's music that leaves your mouth hanging open. Where you can fly and the air smells of freedom.

M: Slavery is what that air smells like. The angels aren't free. They're servants.

AG: Yes, because they choose to be and because they enjoy it. Tell me, can you relate to an intimate conversation where the other person seems to understand you completely? And joy increases with every word?

M: Hideous harmony! Delusion! Praise be to our wild feasts in hell, where we exhaust ourselves rioting and clamoring and getting on each other's nerves.

AG: A hellish noise, I'm sure! I prefer sublime sounds: the roar of a waterfall, or thundering breakers, or the happy shouts of playing children. And in between I love the heavenly calm that floats across the skies like a cloud, allowing us to hear the daffodils sing.

M: I can see I'll have a hard time enticing you with my kind of living.

AG: That's true. Where are you going?

M: (*Getting up*) It's pointless to talk to someone who's as stubborn as you are. What happened to your famous openness? I'm drawn to the comfort of my hell, the smell of self-praise and hypocrisy, of foul compromises and dull instincts. What an aroma!

AG: Is there nothing left in you that longs for the light of a clear morning, when the dew is sparkling and it smells of fresh apples?

Have you never wished you could meet someone who likes you without ulterior motives?

M: There's no such thing. I'm a realist. Reality looks different. And heaven isn't the cozy place you're making it out to be. Everything is transparent, and you can't lie.

AG: We saw during our reader's trip that there are gorgeous apartments there. And if there are apartments, there are also crackling fireplaces filling each room with love. I imagine an early evening in heaven like dark blue velvet spreading out over the angels' houses. They say that the nights haunted by fear were abolished. If there is night at all, it would be a feeling of sparkling stars, a nightly ride on shining unicorns, private conversations beneath a silver moon and a deep, revitalizing sleep.

M: (*On his way out*) No more! Stop your poetic drivel! I won't let you take away my hell.

AG: You're a hopeless case, Mr. M.

M: That may be. At least then I won't have to put any effort into hoping against all reason. What a waste of energy! I love the eternally empty. Goodbye forever!

AG: Thank you so much for . . . Oh! He's disappeared. I guess he was in a hurry.

Bythe

AG: Bythe! Our readers have already gotten to know you as a friendly angel, empathetically guiding a newbie into the other-world. I, however, would also love to know more about your personal life. Some of the things you remarked on *en passant* have somehow stayed with me.

Bythe: Of course, I'm ready. As you know, time is no object for me.

AG: Quite the contrast to Mr. M., who always seems a little rushed.

Bythe: Yes. Heavenly time contains a lot of eternity. In hell, on the other hand, you get the impression that others are stealing your time.

AG: Where do you actually come from, Bythe? Have you always lived in heaven?

Bythe: No, I used to be a human being, but in a different solar system. Then I died and applied for retraining as a guardian angel. It's something I really enjoy doing; I've always had a very caring way with people. That's what I really like about it.

AG: Hold on, you're saying there are more planets in the universe inhabited by human beings?

Bythe: Of course. When you look up at the sky at night, you are also looking at other civilizations. The distances in a three-dimensional universe are—as you probably know—too great to visit each other. But in God's kingdom we have many different human races.

AG: And do they have stories like ours? Did God also become human and . . .

Bythe: *(Laughing)* Oh, no. That's the special thing about you guys. Your world was set apart when redemption took place there. It had an effect on the whole universe, though. We benefit from your story. Just remember, in the letter to the Colossians it is written that God has reconciled everything through Christ—heaven and earth.

AG: Incredible! And did you also have a family?

Bythe: Sure. I had a wife and six children.

AG: And . . . if I may ask a more personal question . . .

Bythe: I don't want to talk about that. God doesn't allow it. It's not supposed to be discussed in detail.

AG: OK. What I can't quite get my head around is that whole guardian angel concept. Is there really always an angel floating around me, constantly influencing me?

Bythe: You have to put it into a greater context: the two worlds are connected. You and your guardian angel have a common mission because your angel is also learning from you.

AG: Really?

Bythe: Yes. Just remember my experiences in the book. Even angels aren't flawless or perfect. Only God is perfect. But we are growing in that direction, like the cherries ripening on the tree in your backyard.

AG: What a strange idea. On earth we call people who are still growing "green."

Bythe: Not bad. Even angels are green to a certain degree. Of course, in comparison with earthly humans angels are far more mature—they have a greater perspective on things, have more experience and foresight, are a hundred times happier, and still keep learning more and more every eternal second. Otherwise, if there wasn't any kind of evolution, life in heaven would be pretty dull.

AG: And how about your moods? I always picture you guys as happy all the time.

Bythe: My moods are actually a lot more balanced than they used to be before I died, that's true. But we also go through changes. For example, when I'm watching one of the children in their sleeping tents being healed from abuse, it gets to me. I'm not made of stone, you know. That's how you can tell when you're feeling real love. At those times, my mood is a little mellower. But afterward there might be a giant party where I meet my friends and we celebrate, and make music, and dance. And that's a good thing. Uninterrupted pure bliss would hardly be blissful to anyone. Think about the house at dusk. Those angels were quite capable of mourning. Real joy feels stronger in contrast.

AG: Yes, I thought about that while reading the book; there's a certain logic to it.

Bythe: Good old John in Revelation thought along those same lines.

AG: How so?

Bythe: He writes about a new creation, that the leaves of the Tree of Life serve to heal the nations. So there are still healing processes happening among us, and that means constant ups and downs. If even God suffers under human sin then it doesn't just bounce off of us, either.

AG: Good. I'd like to come back to this guardian angel thing. Isn't it a little overbearing having angels who are assigned to accompany us and constantly influence our lives? It kind of sounds a little like brainwashing . . .

Bythe: But you're being influenced by all sorts of things, every moment of the day and night: By noise, by commercials, by other people, by your work, by things that happen by chance, by chocolate . . .

AG: Chocolate?

Bythe: Well, yes—chocolate is supposed to lift the spirits. And then there's also the influence of hell. Those guys can get pretty pushy. If there were no angels sending you good thoughts and healing images, you'd be doing much worse. Your inner life has to be balanced out; otherwise you couldn't make decisions in your daily life. Besides, thanks to the angels, no human being is ever truly alone.

AG: Unfortunately, we don't really feel our invisible friends around us.

Bythe: That's OK. God and heaven don't like to be obtrusive. And still the angels in the book of Isaiah sing: "The whole earth is filled with God's glory."

AG: It would help to picture that the next time I'm feeling down. At least now I'm actually glad that angels exist, accompanying us so discreetly. But one more totally different question: Many of my readers are confused when they read something in the Bible about death and resurrection. There are passages where it says that we are resting in our graves until Judgment Day and only then are we raised from the dead. On the other hand, there are several places where it says that we start a new life right after we die—for example, when Jesus says to his neighbor on the cross: "I tell you, today we will meet in paradise." So which version is the right one, then? Does the Bible contradict itself?

Bythe: You know, the Bible isn't a theological encyclopedia of unobjectionable correctness. First and foremost, it's a pastoral book. The first Christians were predominantly made up of two groups: the Jewish Christians and the gentile Christians. Of course, they both had very different backgrounds. For the Jewish Christians, the body had a great significance. They believed earthly life was linked to the body and the soul was connected to our blood. A life after death for them was only conceivable if the body was resurrected, and that was supposed to happen at the end of time.

AG: I see. So you think this idea of lying in your grave for thousands of years and then being resurrected was more for the Jewish Christians?

Bythe: Exactly. The Christians who had more of a Greek heritage found it far easier to imagine an eternal life without their earthly bodies. In their case, the apostle had to emphasize that life without their earthly bodies would still have physical aspects, but with a spiritual body, just like the one that I have.

AG: With which you can eat and drink and dance and embrace your wife and all that. OK, I'm slowly getting it.

Bythe: It's not that hard, is it? Depending on who he was writing to, Paul would try to explain the resurrection in a way that would allow both parties to look forward to it. But he himself knew that he would be where Jesus was as soon as he died. "I would rather die and be with Christ than live," he once wrote to the church in Philippi.

AG: We almost got caught in a theological critique.

Bythe: And that would be a bad thing?

AG: I guess not. In any case, thank you so much for your willingness and openness.

Bythe: Openness is my middle name.

Fictional Reader

AG: Dear fictional reader, after having returned from your little trip to the Beyond, you were standing in front of your bookcase. It later turned out that you hadn't actually died, but rather had a near-death experience. And now you're living your normal life again, without seeing angels, flying around in paradise, or being able to have a conversation with your young grandmother. What are you going to do after this experience? How does someone feel after such an unusual journey?

FR: Good question. I'm still a little dazed. I'm sure I will never really lose my memories of those truly amazing moments. Sometimes, in the middle of my day, I think about that meadow in paradise, or that celebration in the old villa. But even though my desire to return is very strong, almost painful at times, I don't want to go yet.

AG: Why?

FR: Well, I don't know if you'll believe me when I say that somehow I lost my fear of death. Of course, dying itself might still be painful, but that unpleasant feeling that I might fall into a dark, unknown hole has vanished. Now I know that my life here is just the beginning.

AG: I'm particularly interested in knowing whether your daily routine changed at all after your travels to the Beyond. Are you living differently than before?

FR: Hmm, I'll have to think about that. . . . Actually, I think I am living differently than I used to, but I'm not talking about great, revolutionary changes; it's more as if some tracks have been adjusted.

AG: How do you mean?

FR: Well, for example, I sometimes catch myself passing a definite judgment on someone and writing them off. And then this thought enters my mind: "Hold on! Stop! That's a stupid habit. When you get to heaven you won't be able to do that anyhow, to judge people and then pretend you like them."

AG: And what do you do then? Are you completely honest with the person and tell them you've written them off and leave them?

FR: Complete honesty isn't always the best solution. At least I've gotten more cautious with my judgments, because only God truly knows a person. What do I know about who he or she is inside? Then I think, "OK, this guy is a nasty piece of work, but maybe there's also a good side to him . . ."

AG: Have there been other types of adjustments?

FR: Of course. The other day I was feeling really depressed because the things I'd planned didn't work out. And then I thought about all that incredible glory awaiting us in heaven, and the stuff that happened on earth didn't bring me down so much anymore.

AG: So you've become altogether more harmonious? Softer and more relaxed?

FR: You could say that.

AG: But doesn't that seem a little tame? What about some fighting spirit? Did the influence of heaven turn you into a sissy?

FR: *(Laughing)* No, no, not at all. You got the wrong impression. Of course, it's true that I'm now more relaxed about certain things, but I've also become a lot more sensitive to deeds of injustice. It fills me with a . . . a red energy to do something about it.

AG: A red energy? How should I understand that? Does the influence of heaven enrage you?

FR: Rage is the wrong word. It's more a feeling that certain things can't continue, we have to do something about them. Think about Rosa Parks, who started the bus strike in the South by ignoring the racial separation. As a consequence, the civil rights movement developed, later led by Martin Luther King. Or think about the people from Greenpeace who stand up to the destruction of nature. But to be honest, I don't even want to use those extreme kinds of examples. Before, I used to just block out other people's suffering. I felt embarrassed and bothered by the beggars in front of the shops and walked past as fast as I could. Now I look closer and think that something needs to happen.

AG: For example?

FR: Well, I could sit down with the man and talk to him if I have the guts. Or I give him a dollar and kindly look him in the eye. Most people who give something don't even do that. Or if I see that a man in my town is always walking around alone, probably unemployed, and no one ever goes up to him . . .

AG: So heaven basically opened your eyes for the need of others?

FR: Yes. It's weird. I don't really know why. Maybe I breathed in some brotherly love or charity floating around up there and took it back home with me.

AG: OK, but you can't help everyone. That would be total overload.

FR: That's true. But strangely enough, I don't feel the need to help everyone, just those that cross my path or touch my heart. Remember the story of the Good Samaritan. It's not about the man helping everyone who has ever been robbed, just this one man he sees lying on the street.

AG: What else? What other changes has heaven made in your life?

FR: I used to be the kind of person who generally believed that there is something like a God, but that was about it. But after my journey . . . To put it another way: In paradise or in heaven I realized that you can feel God's influence anywhere if you're open to it. And meeting this man who was God, or a human representation of him, that really blew me away. Now, whenever I'm driving my car or riding my bike or soaking in the bathtub, no matter where I am,

I now know that God is always available. I've even caught myself talking to him in my mind, as if he was walking right next to me, like Bythe. So God definitely became a lot more real to me.

AG: I see. Someone once said that heaven is where God is.

FR: Exactly. And then there's this thing that . . . I'm not even sure if I'm on the right track here. Anyhow, something is evolving . . . it's hard to put into words . . .

AG: Give it a try.

FR: It probably sounds really stupid. Another thing that I've still been thinking about a lot and is showing some aftereffects is that scene on the lake when we talked about love and sex.

AG: A fascinating subject.

FR: Absolutely. Before my journey into the Beyond I was convinced that every man secretly wanted to have sex with any woman he found attractive. And that that was normal, a basic masculine trait. Totally standard. Men are a live wire. Deal with it. An instinct you can't fight. Now I think differently about it.

AG: Differently how? Should men flip the off switch or pull the plug?

FR: That wouldn't be a solution. This is more of an intuition. I was pretty impressed that Bythe seems to have lived with one woman for a long time and has formed this very strong bond with her, and that he doesn't feel the need have sex with anyone else. He's completely focused on becoming one with this specific person. And I get the impression that might be how it was supposed to be in the beginning. Now anonymous sex has found its way into our society, and we think that it's completely normal. It's funny, I don't quite know how, but my craving for sex has decreased, as if heavenly love has covered everything . . .

AG: Hmm. The animal kingdom doesn't really practice monogamy, so it does seem to be natural to have several partners.

FR: No, no, there are monogamous species. It doesn't seem unnatural at all. Anyhow, do we really want to adopt animals' lifestyles as our own? In that case we should also make food intake our top priority and spend our whole day chewing and digesting like cows.

AG: Who are you trying to kid? Sexuality is the strongest urge we have, and we shouldn't have to suppress it.

FR: I'm not talking about suppressing it, I'm just saying that it might be meant for one person only. But let's leave it at that. You asked what had *already* changed and I'm really only in the process of forming my opinion on that. I'll have to see how it develops. . . . Another thing that changed for me is the concept of time.

AG: Of course, the clocks in heaven are wired differently.

FR: I used to think that in heaven it's always the present, the here and now, but that's not exactly true.

AG: Right. Because our visit there happened with a kind of chronology, a succession of movements.

FR: And that's how it has to be, otherwise you couldn't do anything, and nothing could develop and grow. It's just that in heaven things don't take a predetermined amount of time. Things take as long as they're supposed to take, without anyone getting impatient. If there were train stations in heaven, there would probably be no time schedule. You'd just depart and arrive on time.

AG: The gospel train is coming . . .

FR: That's what I'd like to learn: to take my time when I'm doing something important and not let it get to me. To close my eyes in the midst of all the hustle and bustle, take a deep breath, and say, "I have all the time in the world." That would be a piece of eternity in my daily life. That's what I want to learn.

AG: Then this trip to the Beyond has adjusted and re-laid quite a few tracks in your life.

FR: You could say that. I'm amazed at how life can change when you start thinking in terms of your goal in the afterlife. To say, "What do I care about heaven? I want to live my life here and now" is ultimately idiocy.

AG: Right, but I don't think that idiocy should have the last word.

FR: All right then, let's end our interview by saying, "See you in heaven."

AG: Exactly.

BIBLIOGRAPHY

From the Bible

Isaiah 11:1–9
Matthew 5:1–10
Luke 23:39–43
Romans 8:18
Philippians 3:20–21
Hebrews 8:5
1 Peter 4:6
Revelation 19:11–15; 20:1–8; 22:1–2

Other Sources

Blum, Wilhelm. *Höhlengleichnisse, von Platon bis Descartes* [Parables from Platon to Descartes]. Bielefeld: Aisthesis Verlag, 2004.

Bieneck-Hagedorn, Andreas. *Ich habe ins Jenseits geblickt* [I Looked into the Afterlife], Neukirchen–Vlyn: Neukirchener Verlagshaus, 2006.

Cardenal, Ernesto. *Das Buch von der Liebe* [The Book of Love]. Wuppertal: Peter-Hammer-Verlag, 1971.

Goethe, Johann Wolfgang von. *Faust*. Trans. A.S. Kline. Poetry in Translation, 2003. www.poetryintranslation.com/PITBR/German/FaustIScenesIVtoVI.htm.

Herzog, Markwart. *Descendus ad Infernos* [Descent into Hell]. Frankfurt: Knecht-Verlag, 1983.

Lewis, C. S. *The Great Divorce*. London: Geoffrey Bles, 1945.
——— . *The Last Battle*. London: The Bodley Head, 1956.

Melzer, Friso. *Sadhu, Sundar, Singh, Leben und Werk. Besonders das Kapitel: Gesichte von der jenseitigen Welt* [Life and Work of Sadhu Sundar Singh, Especially Visions of the Afterlife] Munich: Neubau-Verlag, 1946.

Moody, Raymond A. *Life after Life*. San Francisco: Harper SanFrancisco, 2001.

Rienecker, Fritz. *Das Schönste kommt noch—vom Leben nach dem Sterben* [The Best is Still to Come—about Life after Death]. Wuppertal: Sonne und Schild-Verlag, 1965.

Swedenborg, Emanuel. *De Coelo et Ejus Mirabilibus, et de Inferno, ex Auditis et Visis* [Heaven and Its Wonders, and Hell, from Things Heard and Seen]. London: published by the author, 1758. Published in English as *Heaven and Hell*, trans. George F. Dole. West Chester, PA: Swedenborg Foundation, 2002.

Von Hochheim, Meister Eckhart. *Vom Adel der menschlichen Seele* [About the Glory of the Soul]. Cologne: Anaconda, 1998.

Vorgrimmler, Herbert. *Geschichte der Hölle* [History of Hell]. Munich: Fink Verlag, 1994.